500
superfood dishes

500

superfood dishes

the only compendium of superfood dishes you'll ever need

Beverley Glock

SELLERS

PUBLISHING

A Quintet Book

Published by Sellers Publishing, Inc.
161 John Roberts Road, South Portland, Maine 04106
Visit our Web site: www.sellerspublishing.com
E-mail: rsp@rsvp.com

ISBN: 978-1-4162-4559-9
Library of Congress Control Number: 2014948959
QTT.FHSU

This book was conceived, designed and produced by
Quintet Publishing Limited
4th Floor, Sheridan House
114-116 Western Road
Hove, East Sussex
BN3 1DD

Food Stylist: Beverley Glock
Photographer: Tony Briscoe
Designer: Tania Gomes
Art Director: Michael Charles
Editorial Assistant: Ella Lines
Publishing Assistant: Alice Sambrook
Editorial Director: Emma Bastow
Publisher: Mark Searle

10 9 8 7 6 5 4 3 2 1

Printed in China by 1010 Printing International Ltd.

Disclaimer: As much as we believe in the power of superfoods, the information
in this book is not intended as medical advice, diagnosis, or prescription. You
should always consult a doctor or other health-care professional.

Front cover photograph © 2015 Shutterstock/Stephanie Frey

contents

introduction

Superfoods are foods that are high in nutrients and health giving properties. Eating a diet rich in superfoods should help control your weight; curb hunger pangs, and cravings; protect you from diseases and boost your immune system.

Many superfoods are plant and grain based and the brightest colored fruit and vegetables tend to have the highest concentration of nutrients. To get the most out of eating superfoods try to eat as many different colored fruit and vegetables as you can. Cut down on refined or processed food and sugar and eat whole grains such as brown rice, whole-wheat pasta and bread. Follow the rule of eating colorful food and omit white carbohydrates (white rice, pasta, bread, sugar, or anything with these ingredients in them).

For sweetness swap out sugar and corn syrup for agave nectar or honey, or use dried fruit such as raisins, dates or a little cinnamon or vanilla to sweeten food instead of sugar.

Superfoods are nutritious and delicious and easily adapted to your favorite recipes. Many of the recipes are suitable for vegetarians with alternatives to include meat, poultry, and fish and vice versa.

The following pages contain a list of superfoods and their health giving properties—many of them are everyday foods that you may not have considered to be 'super', and some may be unfamiliar. The important thing with superfood eating is to have fun and experiment with flavors. Healthy eating need never be dull again.

glossary of superfoods

Acai—A red/purple berry from the acai palm tree that grows in Central and South America. Acai is richer in antioxidants than cranberries, raspberries, blackberries, strawberries, or blueberries.

Agave syrup—Agave nectar is a low glycemic index (GI) sweetener from the blue webber agave plant that grows in Mexico and South Africa. It is sweeter than honey and less viscous. Use in place of honey or sugar and store in a dry place away from the sun.

Almonds—Packed with vitamins, minerals, protein, and fiber, almonds make a great addition to any salad or dessert. Almond milk is also a nutritious dairy-free alternative to cow's milk.

Asparagus—Packed with antioxidants, this ranks among the top vegetables for its ability to neutralize free radicals, and it may also help to slow the aging process.

Avocado—Full of good fats which can protect your body against a range of diseases. Avocados have 35 percent more potassium than bananas and are high in vitamin B6, vitamin K, folic acid, and omega 3, 6, and 9.

Bananas—Rich in potassium, fiber, vitamin B6, magnesium and manganese, they strengthen the immune system as they contain cytolcin which is believed to increase white blood cells. Bananas give a natural energy boost and help reduce stress levels as they contain tryptophan, a chemical that converts to the feel-good hormone, seratonin.

Barley—Helps lower cholesterol, use in place of rice and add to vegetable soups.

Beans—Lean protein, high in fiber and B vitamins, eat with brown rice, nuts, and seeds.

Beet—High in folic acid and fiber, manganese and potassium. Eat the greens too, cooked like spinach as they are rich in calcium, iron, and vitamins A and C.

Bell peppers—Eat as many different colors as you can, as they are packed with phytochemicals which help to protect against cancer and neutralize free radicals in the body that damage cells. High in vitamin C and A too.

Blueberries—High in antioxidants, phytochemicals, and flavonoids which help to fight diseases, they also reduce inflammation in the body and can reduce bad cholesterol. Tests show they may reduce the risk of cancer.

Butternut squash—The deep yellow color makes it high in beta carotene, which helps to protect against skin cancer.

Broccoli—See *Cruciferous vegetables*.

Brown rice—A slow-release carbohydrate, with a low GI that helps control blood sugar.

Brown rice syrup—A natural sweetener with a nutty flavor, half as sweet as sugar.

Cheese—Feta, goat, and parmesan are high in calcium.

Cherries—A low-calorie fruit that is pigment-rich, helping protect against cancer and neurological diseases. High in antioxidant melatonin, which is a feel-good hormone.

Chia seeds—The richest source of plant-based omega 3 fatty acids, loaded with antioxidants,

high in protein, minerals, and fiber. Chia seeds swell to more than 5 times their weight in liquid so they'll help make you feel full quicker and can help with weight loss.

Chickpeas—Rich in vitamin B6 and thought to help premenstrual stress (PMS) and menopausal symptoms, while also helping cardiovascular health.

Chlorella—A single-celled green algae that contains the highest amount of chlorophyll in any edible plant. It's used to increase "good bacteria" in the gut to improve digestion and to help treat ulcers, Crohn's disease, and diverticulosis. Chlorella is used to prevent cancer and helps reduce radiation treatment side effects by stimulating the immune system and increasing white blood counts. It also helps to slow the aging process.

Chocolate/raw cacao—Dairy-free 70 percent cocoa or higher elevates your mood, improves your blood flow, and can lower blood pressure. It helps reduce inflammation and bad cholesterol and contains heaps of antioxidants. Raw cacao is even better as none of the nutrients are lost in heat treatment, so make up your own raw chocolates instead. Raw cacao contains more antioxidants than acai, goji berries, or blueberries.

Cinnamon—Stabilizes blood sugar levels and encourages blood flow through the body.

Coconut oil—Quickly and easily absorbed by the body, it's an easy energy source that may help you burn more fat. It helps protect against heart disease and lowers cholesterol slightly. It is excellent for cooking as it does not form harmful trans fats when heated even at high temperatures. Use in place of butter and oil in cooking. Add a pinch of salt to savory recipes to reduce the coconut flavor.

Cranberries—High in vitamins C and D, potassium, and iron, raw cranberries can help protect against cancer and help to bolster the immune system.

Cruciferous vegetables—Including broccoli, Brussels sprouts, cauliflower, cabbage, kale, and bok choy, these all help to lower your cancer risk as they have the ability to inhibit the growth of cancer cells and reduce the production of free radicals.

Cumin—Contains anti-inflammatory properties and also helps reduce bloating.

Dates—Very high in fiber, dates help to reduce inflammation and contain antioxidants. They are also high in iron, and are a great alternative sweet fix to sugar.

Eggplant—High in fiber, low in fat, they help reduce bad cholesterol and high blood pressure.

Eggs—Fabulously high in protein and vitamin D to protect and bolster the immune system, eat eggs for breakfast to help control your appetite for the rest of the day.

Garlic—Anti-viral and good for reducing bad cholesterol.

Ginger—Thought to have anti-inflammatory properties and help with arthritis.

Goji berries—Also known as Wolfberry, these are native to China. Rich in vitamin A to help protect against skin cancer. High in antioxidants and complex starches that benefit the immune system.

Greek yogurt—An excellent source of calcium, potassium, protein, zinc, and vitamins B6 and B12. It contains probiotic cultures and is lower in lactose with twice the protein of regular yogurts. Eat Greek yogurt with fresh berries instead of low-fat fruit yogurt, which is packed with sugar.

Green tea/matcha—This is very high in antioxidants and thought to help fat burning.

Hemp—A good source of protein, especially for vegans, contains omega 3 and 6 fatty acids and is thought to be energy boosting.

Leafy green vegetables—See *Cruciferous vegetables*. Alternatively add spirulina, wheatgrass, or chlorella powder to your food daily.

Linseeds—also known as flaxseed, are a great vegetarian source of the omega 3 essential fatty acids, especially in ground form.

Lucuma powder—A sweet, low-GI alternative to sugar in baking and cooking that is packed with antioxidants, vitamins, and minerals. Thought to have beneficial effects on skin aging. Use lucuma powder to sweeten instead of sugar. Lucuma fruit are native to Peru.

Maca powder—The root of the maca plant, native to Peru and thought to boost energy and enhance athletic performance. Also good for helping with menopausal symptoms and reducing stress and depression.

Mackerel—Oily fish packed with omega 3 fatty acids.

Mango— Mangoes are high in beta carotene, which helps to protect against skin cancer.

Miso—Rich in amino acids, great for reducing cholesterol and PMS symptoms.

Nuts—High in calcium, zinc, and good fats, great for supporting the immune system and keeping skin healthy.

Oats—These naturally lower cholesterol and are high in fiber and vitamin B, use gluten-free oats for gluten-free dietary requirements.

Olives/olive oil—High in oleic acid, which helps to keep the cardiovascular system healthy.

Onions—Anti-inflammatory, anti-cholesterol, with antioxidant properties.

Oysters—A well known aphrodisiac as they contain more zinc per serving than any other food. Zinc is a key mineral and deficiency can lead to impotence in men. Oysters are low in fat, a good source of proteins and are high in omega 3 fatty acids, potassium, magnesium, and vitamin E.

Pink grapefruit—High in vitamin C and lycopene, which is a carotinoid and thought to help protect the prostate gland.

Pistachios—Colorful and tasty, these nuts are rich in mono-unsaturated fatty acids and an excellent source of antioxidants.

Pomegranate—Middle Eastern fruit of which we eat the seeds. Helps prevent heart disease and unclog arteries. It can also help inhibit viral infections and thought to reduce the progress of prostate cancer.

Pumpkin/pumpkin seeds—High in zinc, which helps you recover from colds quicker and is also good for treating acne.

Quinoa—A South American seed that is high in protein and a great alternative to starchy foods such as rice, pasta, and couscous. It also releases energy very slowly, keeping your blood sugar levels stable.

Raspberries—High levels of phytochemicals to protect and fight against cancer, plus they help to slow down signs of aging.

Salmon—A rich source of protein and essential fatty acids plus vitamins and minerals to help protect against cancer, macular degeneration, depression, and cognitive decline, line-caught wild Alaska salmon is the best.

Soy/tofu—Great for easing menopausal symptoms, high in calcium and a good alternative to dairy.

Spelt—An ancient wheat with a slightly nutty flavor that can be used in recipes instead of standard wheat flour. If you are intolerant of wheat you may be able to eat spelt, although spelt contains gluten so it's not suitable for people with gluten allergies, intolerances, or with celiac disease.

Spirulina—A blue/green algae from saltwater lakes in Africa and Mexico. It is high in B vitamins, calcium and iron which help stimulate the metabolism and reduce tiredness. It is thought to help prevent cancer, fight off infections, and help counter allergies such as hay fever.

Stevia—A sugar substitute extracted from the leaves of the plant species Stevia rebaudiana.

Strawberries—High levels of phytochemicals to protect and fight against cancer, plus they help to slow down signs of aging. Fresh strawberries are an excellent source of vitamin C.

Sunflower seeds—High in calcium, selenium, and zinc.

Sweet potatoes—Rich in beta carotene, antioxidants, and helps reduce inflammation.

Tahini/sesame seeds—High in calcium, selenium, thiamin, and zinc.

Tomatoes—High in lycopene and vitamin C.

Tuna—Oily fish packed with omega 3 fatty acids, fresh tuna has higher quantities than canned.

Walnuts—Just a few walnuts will give you your daily recommended dose of omega 3 plus they are fantastic for helping protect your brain against Alzheimer's and Parkinson's disease.

Wheatgrass—This is young grass of the wheat plant so it is not suitable for those with wheat allergies or intolerances. High in chlorophyll and helps to combat colds, coughs, digestive ailments, and some skin conditions as it is a natural detoxifyer.

Whole-grain pasta/bread—Low GI with slow-release carbohydrates, so eating the whole grain helps keep you fuller for longer. It will also fill you up more quickly than eating white pasta and bread and contains more vitamins and minerals.

breakfast

There's no better time of the day to enjoy
superfoods than in the morning. A great way to
begin your day is with a wholesome breakfast.

berry bircher muesli

see variations page 34

The ultimate breakfast, full of oats, fruit, yogurt, nuts, and seeds. Each mouthful feels like it's doing you good. Prepare the base the night before and leave it to chill in the refrigerator adding the chopped fruit each morning. It will keep for 2–3 days in the refrigerator without the fruit.

1 3/4 cups rolled oats
1 cup freshly pressed apple juice
1 tbsp. runny honey or agave nectar
4 tbsp. Greek yogurt
4 apples, grated with skin on

1/3 cup raisins
2 tbsp. pumpkin seeds
2 1/2 cups strawberries, chopped
1 3/4 cups raspberries
1 tbsp. goji berries

Put the oats in a large bowl and drizzle over most of the juice, mix well, adding the rest of the juice if the oats are dry. They should be wet but not sloppy. Stir in the honey or agave, yogurt, grated apple, raisins, and pumpkin seeds. This is your base.

When you're ready to serve or eat the muesli, stir in the strawberries and raspberries, and sprinkle the goji berries over the top.

Serves 4–6

pancakes

see variations page 35

Classic fluffy pancakes with a superfood twist, using different flours and a version that is egg-free. Serve with blueberry compote for a healthy superfood breakfast.

1 cup buckwheat flour
2 eggs
1 tbsp. rice syrup, agave, or maple syrup
1 tsp. vanilla extract
3 tbsp. buttermilk
1/2 cup, plus 2 tbsp. almond, soy, or dairy milk
a little butter or coconut oil

Syrup:
1 3/4 cups blueberries
2 tbsp. rice or agave syrup

Put the flour in a mixing bowl and make a well in the centre. Break the eggs into a small bowl, beat lightly and pour into the well, add the vanilla and buttermilk. Start to mix, gradually drawing in the flour from around the edges, adding the almond, soy, or dairy milk when the mixture starts to thicken. Keep mixing until all the flour has been incorporated. The batter should be a thick dropping consistency, add a little more milk if it's too thick.

Heat a knob of butter or a little coconut oil in a non-stick skillet, pour 1 1/2 tablespoons of the batter into the skillet, gently flattening the mixture to a "round." Cook for a few minutes until you see bubbles on the surface, flip the pancake and cook the other side for a few minutes until light golden brown. Transfer to a warm plate and cover with aluminum foil to keep warm. Repeat with the rest of the mixture. Heat the blueberries and syrup in a saucepan over a low to medium heat, cook for 5–10 minutes until the fruit collapses and serve poured over the pancakes.

Makes 12 pancakes

quinoa porridge

see variations page 36

Quinoa is one of the super superfoods. South Americans have known this for a long time but it's taken time for the rest of the world to catch on. Quinoa is gluten-free, it's not actually a grain but a seed and contains all 9 essential amino acids. It's easy to prepare and digest and is a good alternative to rice and couscous. Rinse it well in water to remove any bitter coating left after processing, then cook in 1 part quinoa to 3 parts liquid for 15–20 minutes. It will increase in volume by around 4 times and become almost translucent and fluffy.

1/3 cup quinoa
3/4 cup almond milk, plus extra to serve
1 tsp. ground cinnamon
2 tsp. vanilla extract
1 tbsp. linseed

2 apples, cored and grated with skins on
2 tbsp. raisins
2 tbsp. agave syrup or honey
1 tbsp. goji berries
1 tbsp. shelled pistachios, roughly chopped

Rinse the quinoa thoroughly, put in a saucepan with the milk, cinnamon, and vanilla, bring to a boil, cover, and simmer for 15–20 minutes until the liquid has been absorbed and the quinoa is "al dente."

Remove from the heat, stir, and mix in the linseed, grated apples, raisins, and half the agave syrup or honey. Stir and serve with the goji berries and pistachios scattered on top with a drizzle of the remaining agave syrup.

Serves 2–3

chocolate chia pudding

see variations page 37

Yes, you can still have chocolate pudding and eat healthily. Packed full of antioxidants, raw cacao is the unprocessed version of cocoa so it hasn't been exposed to any chemical processing and drying that destroys a lot of the nutrients. Raw cacao has up to 40 times the antioxidants of blueberries. It is the highest plant-based source of iron and one of the highest plant-based sources of magnesium for a healthy heart.

1/2 cup chia seeds
1 cup almond milk
4 tbsp. agave syrup or honey or 1 tbsp.
   powdered stevia
2–3 tbsp. raw cacao powder

1 tsp. vanilla extract
1/2 cup fresh raspberries
toasted, slivered almonds to serve

Begin the night before and soak the chia seeds in the almond milk. Add the agave syrup (or honey or powdered stevia if using) and mix until dissolved.

Stir in the cacao and mix well with a fork. It will take time but keep stirring and gradually it will all incorporate. Stir in the vanilla extract, cover and chill in the refrigerator overnight.

In the morning the seeds will have swelled and look like tiny balls. Taste and adjust the sweetness, adding a little more agave, honey, stevia or cacao if needed. To serve, layer some of the raspberries and chocolate chia in a glass and serve with a few raspberries on the top sprinkled with toasted slivered almonds.

Serves 4

granola

see variations page 38

This delicious nutrient-packed granola is lovely served with fresh berries and Greek yogurt or just eaten as a snack.

2 cups rolled oats
3/4 cup sunflower seeds
3/4 cup pumpkin seeds
1/4 cup chia seeds
1/4 cup linseeds
3/4 cup whole almonds, roughly chopped
1/2 cup whole hazelnuts, roughly chopped
1/2 cup Brazil nuts, roughly chopped
1/2 cup pecan nuts, roughly chopped

1/4 cup, plus 1 tbsp. rice or agave syrup
1/4 cup maple syrup
1/2 cup coconut oil
1 tsp. ground cinnamon
1/2 cup flame raisins
1/2 cup golden raisins
1/4 cup dried blueberries
1/4 cup goji berries

Preheat the oven to 325°F (160°C).

Put the oats, seeds, and roughly chopped nuts in a large bowl. Put the syrups and coconut oil in a small saucepan and gently warm to mix and loosen the syrup. Pour over the dry mixture, sprinkle over the cinnamon and stir well to mix.

Transfer to a lined cookie sheet and bake for 20–30 minutes until golden and toasted, mixing up the granola halfway through to ensure it browns evenly. Allow to cool, stir in the dried fruit and store in an airtight container.

Serves 4–6

fruit smoothie

see variations page 40

This delicious smoothie is a perfect breakfast on the go.

1 tbsp. blueberries
1 tbsp. strawberries, hulled
    and sliced
1 tbsp. frozen raspberries
1 tbsp. frozen black currants

3 Brazil nuts, chopped
1/2 cup Greek yogurt
pinch cinnamon
2 tsp. agave or rice syrup
1 tsp. acai powder

3 ice cubes
coconut water or almond milk

Put all the ingredients in a blender and blend until smooth, adding additional coconut water or almond milk if the mixture is too thick.

Serves 1

green smoothie

see variations page 39

This is one of those ideal pick-me-up smoothies that you'll reach for after a late night.

handful of kale, chopped and stalks removed
3 kiwi fruit, peeled and diced
3/4-in. fresh gingerroot, grated
1 apple, peeled, cored and sliced
1/2 cucumber, diced

1/2 cup coconut water or water
1 tsp. spirulina, wheatgrass, or chlorella powder
4 ice cubes

Put all the ingredients in a blender and blend well.

Serves 1

smoked salmon & scrambled eggs

see variations page 41

This is one of the simplest everyday superfoods. Serve on seeded rye or sourdough bread, lightly toasted with a pinch of spirulina, chlorella, or matcha green tea for an additional superfood boost.

1 tbsp. butter
4 free-range eggs, lightly beaten
sea salt and freshly ground black pepper

2 slices smoked salmon, torn into pieces
2 slices seeded rye or sourdough bread, lightly
  toasted, to serve

Heat the butter in a saucepan, pour in the beaten eggs, season lightly, and stir until just starting to solidify. Add the smoked salmon pieces, and keep stirring until almost set. Remove from the heat and serve on the toast.

Serves 2

brown rice kedgeree

see variations page 42

An Indian dish brought to the United Kingdom by returning British colonials, kedgeree is a breakfast dish that, in the days before refrigeration, transformed yesterday's leftovers into a filling and healthy breakfast.

1 cup whole-grain basmati rice
sunflower or hemp oil
1 large onion, chopped
2-in. fresh ginger root, grated
1 garlic clove, finely chopped
2 tsp. madras curry powder
1 tbsp. mustard seeds
juice of 2 lemons

2 tomatoes, chopped
1 fresh red chile, deseeded and chopped
1 lb smoked mackerel fillets
1/2 cup frozen peas, defrosted
2 large free-range eggs, hard-boiled
1 bunch fresh cilantro, chopped

Cook the rice, drain, rinse under cold running water and drain again. Heat the oil and fry the onion gently over a low heat for around 10 minutes so it softens and gently colors rather than browns. Stir in the ginger and garlic and cook for a further 2 minutes. Stir in the curry powder and mustard seeds and cook for 2–3 minutes until fragrant. Add the cooked rice and stir well to coat the rice with the spices.

Add the lemon juice, tomatoes and chopped chile, stir to mix. Break the mackerel fillets into pieces, removing the skin, and stir into the rice. Add the peas and cook for a few minutes until hot. Cut the hard-boiled eggs into quarters and stir in gently along with the fresh cilantro.

Serves 4–6

quinoa breakfast muffins

see variations page 43

These are delicious and shouldn't be relegated to breakfast unless you allow yourself to eat breakfast at any time of day. The quinoa is fabulous and gives the muffins a "nutty" texture. Really good, and dairy-free too.

2 cups cooked quinoa
2 medium eggs
1 cup almond milk
5 tbsp. agave or honey or 1/2 cup light
    muscovado sugar
1/4 cup coconut oil, warmed
2 tsp. vanilla extract
1/2 cup oatmeal or rolled oats
3/4 cup spelt flour
2 tsp. baking powder

3 tsp. ground cinnamon
zest of 2 oranges
1/2 cup chopped Brazil nuts
1 apple, peeled and diced
1/2 cup raisins
1/2 cup unsweetened shredded coconut
1 1/2 cups fresh raspberries
1 tbsp. coconut sugar
1 tsp. ground cinnamon, to finish

Preheat the oven to 375°F (190°C).

Mix together the quinoa, eggs, almond milk, agave, coconut oil, and vanilla extract. In a separate bowl, mix together the oatmeal, flour, baking powder, cinnamon, orange zest, Brazil nuts, apple, raisins, and coconut. Mix the dry ingredients with the wet ingredients and stir well. Gently stir in the raspberries, being careful not to crush them. Fill 12–15 muffin cases in a muffin pan. Mix together the coconut sugar and cinnamon, and spinkle over each muffin. Bake for 20–25 minutes until golden brown and springy to the touch. Leave to cool before eating.

Makes 12–15 muffins

variations

berry bircher muesli

see base recipe page 19

summer berry
Replace the raisins with dried cherries and reduce the strawberries to
1 cup, add 1 cup blueberries, 1 cup red currants and 1 cup blackberries.

pear & orange
Add the zest of 2 oranges and replace the apple juice with the juice of 3–4
oranges. Replace the grated apple with grated pear, replace the raisins with
dried cranberries, omit the berries and add 3–4 segmented clementines,
satsumas, or oranges.

nuts & seeds
Reduce the pumpkin seeds to 1 tablespoon, add 1 tablespoon sunflower
seeds, 1 tablespoon chopped Brazil nuts and 1 tablespoon chopped
hazelnuts.

pomegranate
Replace the apple juice with pomegranate juice, the raisins with cranberries
and the berries with the seeds of two pomegranates. Add 2 tablespoons
chopped pistachios and drizzle with a little rose water and a few whole
pistachios just before serving.

variations

pancakes

see base recipe page 20

egg-free
Omit the eggs, replace with 2 tablespoons chia seeds soaked in 6 tablespoons water for 5 minutes until thickened, proceed with main recipe.

spelt pancakes
Replace the buckwheat flour with the same quantity of whole-grain or white spelt flour.

banana pancakes
Add 1 ripe mashed banana to the pancake batter at the same time as the eggs.

blueberry & acai pancakes
Add 1 cup whole, crushed blueberries and 1 teaspoon acai powder to the batter just before cooking.

with strawberry compote
Replace the blueberries with the same quantity of sliced strawberries, cook very gently to avoid the strawberries falling apart.

variations

quinoa porridge

see base recipe page 21

rose quinoa porridge

Add 1 teaspoon rose water and stir in just before serving, sprinkle with a few
dried rose petals to give it a Middle Eastern flavor.

spiced coconut porridge

Add 1 tablespoon shredded coconut, 1 tablespoon grated or crumbled
creamed coconut, 1 star anise, 4 cardamom pods and 1/2 teaspoon ground
ginger to the quinoa and milk mixture. To serve, stir in 1–2 teaspoons
coconut cream with the agave, berries, and pistachios scattered on top as in
the main recipe.

cranberries, cherries & amaranth porridge

Reduce the quinoa by 1 tablespoon and cook with 1 tablespoon amaranth.
Replace the raisins with 1 teaspoon dried cranberries plus 1 tablespoon dried
cherries. Omit the goji berries and top with chopped fresh cherries or other
berries.

chocolate banana porridge

Omit the raisins. Replace the goji berries with a sliced banana and the
pistachios with 6–8 chopped Brazil nuts, sprinkle with a few dark chocolate
chips to serve.

variations

smoked salmon & scrambled eggs

see base recipe page 28

with wilted spinach
Lightly steam two handfuls of fresh spinach, and stir into the eggs with the smoked salmon.

with kale
Chop 1/2 cup fresh kale, removing the thick stalks, steam lightly and add to the eggs with the smoked salmon.

with sun-dried tomatoes & olives
Drain and slice 4 sun-dried tomatoes and 6 black olives, add to the eggs with the smoked salmon.

brown rice kedgeree

see base recipe page 31

with salmon
Replace the mackerel fillets with poached salmon fillets, flaked.

with quinoa
Replace the rice with the same quantity of quinoa, cooked as instructed on the package.

with barley
Replace the rice with the same quantity of barley, cook as instructed on the package. Barley takes longer to cook than rice so allow a longer cooking time.

quinoa breakfast muffins

see base recipe page 32

gluten-free quinoa breakfast muffins
Replace the oatmeal with gluten-free oats, the spelt flour with gluten-free flour, baking powder with gluten-free baking powder, and add 1 teaspoon xanthan gum.

chocolate banana muffins
Omit the orange zest, Brazil nuts, apple, raisins, and coconut and replace with 1/2 cup raw dark chocolate chips and 3 ripe mashed bananas.

red berry & hazelnut muffins
Omit the Brazil nuts, apple, raisins, and coconut and replace with 1 cup fresh pitted cherries, halved, 1/2 cup dried cranberries or cherries and 1/2 cup chopped roasted hazelnuts.

rhubarb, orange & pecan muffins
Replace the Brazil nuts with chopped pecans, omit the apple, raisins and coconut and replace with 1 cup chopped fresh rhubarb.

snacks & appetizers

Snacks and appetizers are often the guilty pleasures

of our day, but there are many other healthy

choices. These recipes give you some tasty options.

beet & walnut hummus

see variations page 62

Beets and walnuts give an extra depth to hummus as well as additional nutrients and antioxidants. Serve with a selection of raw vegetables or warm pita.

1/2 cup walnuts, chopped
14-oz. can chickpeas, drained and rinsed
3-4 cooked beets, chopped
1 garlic clove, crushed

juice of 1-2 lemons
1 tbsp tahini
sea salt and pepper to taste

Heat a heavy skillet until smoking hot, add the walnuts and dry fry for 2-3 minutes until they release their aroma and begin to darken in patches. Transfer to a food processor.

Add the remaining ingredients, leaving a few walnuts to decorate, and blend until smooth, add a little more lemon juice if the mixture is too thick.

Serve with some walnuts scattered on top, if desired.

Serves 4-6

beet falafel with tahini sauce

see variations page 63

Beets are excellent for helping to lower blood pressure. This recipe makes a wonderful healthy lunch and it keeps well in the refrigerator for a few days.

1 tsp. coriander seeds
1 tsp. cumin seeds
14-oz. can chickpeas, drained and rinsed
1 raw beet, peeled and grated
juice of 1 lemon
1 fresh red chile, deseeded and finely chopped
1 garlic clove, chopped
1 tbsp. fresh cilantro, chopped
2–3 tbsp. whole-grain breadcrumbs—optional,
    omit for gluten-free version

natural yogurt, to serve
sea salt and freshly ground black pepper
4 whole-grain pita breads to serve with salad

Tahini sauce:
1 tbsp. tahini paste
juice of 1 lemon
2–3 tbsp. water

Put the coriander seeds and cumin seeds in a dry skillet, set over a high heat and cook for 1–2 minutes, shaking the skillet all the time, until the spices release their aroma. Be careful they don't burn. Transfer the spices to a pestle and mortar or spice grinder and roughly grind. Transfer to a food processor.

Add all the other ingredients except the breadcrumbs and yogurt and process until ground but not pureed. Stir the breadcrumbs into the mixture and form into walnut-sized balls. Place in the refrigerator to firm up for 1 hour.

Preheat the oven to 350°F (180°C). Transfer the falafel to a greased cookie sheet. Bake for 10–15 minutes until dark red and cooked through.

To make the tahini sauce, mix all the ingredients together, adding sufficient water to make a dropping consistency.

Warm the pitas, then slice them open, stuff with salad, share the falafel between them, drizzle with yogurt and tahini, and eat warm.

Serves 4

crunchy roasted chickpeas

see variations page 64

This is such a simple and easy dish to make, and you can serve it as an alternative to chips or as a side dish for a curry or stuff into a whole-grain pita bread with some falafel and salad.

14-oz. can chickpeas, drained and rinsed
1 tbsp. olive oi
1 tsp. ground cumin
1 tsp. ground coriander
1 tsp. sweet paprika

1 tsp. hot chili powder
1 tsp. freshly ground black pepper
1 tsp. sea salt
large pinch of sugar

Preheat the oven to 400°F (200°C).

Pat dry the chickpeas on paper towels and spread on a cookie sheet in a single layer. Drizzle with olive oil and sprinkle with the remaining ingredients. The best way to achieve good coverage so the spices don't clump is to hold the spoon high over the cookie sheet and tap the handle with your other hand, the higher you hold the spoon the best sprinkling coverage you'll achieve.

Mix everything with your hands and roast for 15 minutes, shake, and roast for another 10–15 minutes, until the chickpeas are golden brown and crispy. They should be crispy all the way through, if they are soft in the middle, cook for a little longer. Let cool then store in an airtight container for 2–3 days to keep crisp. If they become soft, roast for a few minutes before serving to crisp them up again.

Serves 4

kale chips

see variations page 65

A superfood alternative to potato chips and tortilla chips. Super healthy, packed full of nutrients, and a fraction of the fat of chips, they are a delicious, crispy, low-carb, low-calorie snack alternative. They are also great to serve as nibbles at parties.

1 bunch of kale
1 tbsp. olive or coconut oil
1 tsp. sea salt

Preheat the oven to 350°F (180°C). Line a cookie sheet with baking parchment.

Remove the stems from the kale leaves, and tear the leaves into 2-in. pieces. Wash and dry the kale in a salad spinner or pat dry on clean paper towels. Place the kale in a bowl, drizzle over the oil and mix well with your hands. Transfer to the cookie sheet in a single layer and sprinkle over the sea salt.

Bake for 8–15 minutes, checking them regularly, the edges should just start to brown and you may need to remove some that have cooked more quickly and put the rest in for a little longer. Be careful as they burn easily.

Remove from the oven and leave on the cookie sheet for 5 minutes to allow the chips to crisp up a little more. Serve right away. They will keep in an airtight container but will lose their crispness, refresh in the oven for a few minutes just before serving.

Serves 4

aduki bean dip

see variations page 66

Serve with a selection of raw vegetables or pita chips (see page 54).

14-oz. can aduki beans
1 tbsp. tahini paste
juice of 1 lemon
1 garlic clove, crushed
3–4 tbsp. extra virgin olive oil
1 tbsp. toasted sesame seeds

Put all the ingredients, except the sesame seeds, in a food processor and process until smooth. Alternatively, mash with a potato masher for a less smooth version. Chill until ready to serve, then sprinkle with the toasted sesame seeds.

Serves 4–6

sprouted sunflower seeds hummus

see variations page 67

Begin the day before by soaking the sunflower seeds in water. The water will have an odd green tinge the next day, just drain and rinse the seeds well.

1 cup sunflower seeds, soaked for 24 hours in
    water, drained and rinsed
2 garlic cloves, finely chopped
2 tbsp. tahini
juice of 2 limes

1/4 tsp. garam masala
1 tbsp. extra virgin olive oil
pinch of sea salt
crudites or seeded bread, to serve

Put all the ingredients in a food processor and blend to a puree. Serve with a selection of crudites or with some seeded bread.

Serves 4

whole-grain pita chips

see variations page 68

A healthy, very easy-to-make version of tortilla chips. The chips keep well in an airtight container for 1 week.

1 pack of whole-grain pita breads
olive oil spray
hummus and dips, to serve

Toast the pita breads under a hot broiler for 2–3 minutes until they begin to puff up. Remove from the broiler and carefully split the pita bread in two with the tip of a sharp knife (be careful as you cut into the pita as the hot air inside could burn). Separate the two halves so you have two thin oval pita breads. Use a pair of kitchen scissors to cut each oval into 6–8 triangles.

Preheat the oven to 425°F (220°C). Lay the pita triangles on a greased cookie sheet, spray with a little olive oil and bake until they are crisp and golden. The thicker triangles will take longer than the thinner ones so you may need to remove some before others are cooked. Transfer to a cooling rack and let them cool fully before storing in an airtight container to keep them crisp.

Serve with hummus and other dips.

Serves 4

tapenade

see variations page 69

This fabulously tasty and versatile dip can be used to create a salad dressing with the addition of extra oil and a little lemon juice, or drizzled on vegetables before roasting. Serve on toasted sourdough bread as an appetizer or with breadsticks and crudites as a dip.

3 1/2 oz. jar pitted black olives
1 garlic clove, chopped
zest and juice of 1 lemon
1 tbsp. extra virgin olive oil

Drain the olives and rinse them thoroughly. Add to a food processor with the garlic, lemon zest and juice. Blend, adding the olive oil in a stream while the mixture is pureeing. Once it becomes a thick, grainy paste it's ready.

Cover and chill in the refrigerator until needed.

Serves 4–6

guacamole

see variations page 70

Homemade guacamole is delicious and easy to adapt to personal tastes. You can make it as chunky or as smooth as you prefer.

1 ripe avocado
Juice of 1 lime
a little chili powder or paprika

Halve the avocado, remove the stone, scoop out the flesh and chop into chunks. Add the lime juice and mash to the consistency you prefer. If you like it really smooth, then use an immersion blender. Sprinkle with a little chili powder or paprika to serve.

Serves 4

cucumber tarts with smoked oysters & cream cheese

see variations page 71

Gluten-free, low-carb, high protein, high in nutrients, the ultimate canapé and a great talking point for health conscious friends. Smoked oysters in cans sounds a little odd but trust me, mixed with the cream cheese and lemon juice they are divine.

1 cucumber, washed
3-oz. can smoked oysters in oil, drained
3/4 cup cream cheese

juice of 2 lemons
sea salt and freshly ground black pepper

Slice the cucumber into 2-in. pieces and use a teaspoon to scoop out most of the watery seed center, making sure you leave a little to hold the filling. This will act as your "tart" case. If you scoop all of the center out the filling will fall straight through as you attempt to pick it up.

To make the filling, whizz the remaining ingredients together in a food processor until smooth. Taste and add more lemon juice if required.

To serve, place teaspoonfuls of the filling into the center indent of the cucumber slices, chill and serve.

Serves 4

spicy cashew nuts

see variations page 72

Healthier to nibble on than chips and candy, cashew nuts, along with other nuts, are high in omega 3 fatty acids and minerals such as iron, magnesium, and zinc.

3 cups cashew nuts
1 tbsp. sunflower or olive oil
1 tsp. cumin seeds
1 tsp. coriander seeds

1 tsp. sea salt flakes
1 tsp. chili flakes
1 tsp. coconut sugar or palm sugar

Grind the cumin, coriander, salt, chili flakes, and sugar in a pestle and mortar until you have a rough paste. Heat the oil in a sillter or wok, add the cashew nuts and stir-fry for 1-2 minutes. Add the paste to the skillet and stir-fry for another minute until fragrant and well coated.

Drain on paper towels and let cool, store in an airtight container for up to a week.

Serves 4

cheewra

see variations page 73

Nuts and seeds with an Indian twist, delicious for snacking.

sunflower oil, for deep frying
1 cup cashew nuts
1 cup unsalted peanuts
3 tbsp. golden raisins
3 tbsp. roasted chickpeas (see page 48)
1 tbsp. black mustard seeds
1 tbsp. sesame seeds

1/2 tsp. ground turmeric
1/2 tsp. ground black pepper
pinch ground cloves
1/2 tsp. ground cinnamon
1 tsp. sea salt
1 1/2 tsp. superfine sugar

Heat the sunflower oil in a deep wok or saucepan, you'll need it around 2 in. (5 cm.) deep. Test that it's hot enough by carefully dropping a nut, it should begin to bubble immediately.

Deep-fry the cashew nuts first, stirring them and scooping them out with a slotted spoon once they are golden brown. Drain well on lots of paper towels. Repeat with the peanuts and then with the golden raisins. Once drained and patted with paper towels to remove most of the oil, transfer to a bowl. Add the roasted chickpeas.

Heat 1 tablespoon of oil in a small skillet, add the mustard seeds and sesame seeds. Once they begin to pop, add the turmeric and stir quickly to mix, remove from the heat and add to the bowl with the nuts to serve.

Add the rest of the ingredients, stir well to mix and let cool. Serve.

Serves 4

variations

beet & walnut hummus

see base recipe page 45

beet and cashew nut hummus
Replace the walnuts with the same quantity of cashew nuts, cook as before.

roasted bell pepper and walnut hummus
Replace the beet with 2 roasted bell peppers from a jar, drained, cook as before.

harissa hummus
Add 1-2 teaspoons rose harissa paste (depending on how hot you like it).

roasted onion hummus
Omit the beet and walnuts. Thinly slice a large onion, saute in olive oil for 10-15 minutes over a low heat until soft but not browned, add 1 teaspoon sweet paprika, pinch of cayenne, 1/2 teaspoon ground cumin, 1/2 teaspoon ground cilantro and cook for 2-3 minutes until the spices release their aroma. Blend as before leaving a few onions to decorate the top of the hummus and sprinkle with a few sesame seeds.

beet falafel with tahini sauce

see base recipe page 46

cilantro falafel
Omit the beet and add 2 tablespoons chopped fresh cilantro, proceed with main recipe.

spinach falafel
Omit the beet and add 2 cups fresh spinach, proceed with main recipe.

harissa falafel
Omit the beet and add 1 tablespoon rose harissa, the grated zest of a lime, 1 tablespoon chopped fresh cilantro and a pinch of allspice.

lima bean falafel
Omit the beet, replace with 1 cup skinless lima beans, these will give the falafel a lovely green color.

variations

crunchy roasted chickpeas

see base recipe page 48

wasabi chickpeas
Omit the paprika and chili powder and sprinkle 1–2 teaspoons wasabi powder over the beans, mix well and roast as in main recipe.

soy chickpeas
Replace the olive oil with sesame oil, omit the cumin, ground coriander, paprika, and chili powder and drizzle with 1 tablespoon dark soy sauce. Sprinkle over 2 teaspoons Chinese five spice powder.

curry chickpeas
Replace the olive oil with coconut oil and the cumin, ground coriander, paprika and chili powder with 2 teaspoons madras curry powder.

coconut & kale
Replace the olive oil with coconut oil, cook as in main recipe. Toast 1/4 cup dried shredded coconut in a dry skillet for a few minutes until golden brown and fragrant. Stir into the roasted chickpeas along with one portion of kale chips (see page 51).

coconut & cinnamon
Replace the olive oil with coconut oil, omit the spices and replace with 2 teaspoons ground cinnamon and 2 tablespoons coconut sugar.

variations

kale chips

see base recipe page 51

chili
Stir in 1 teaspoon chili powder or dried crushed chiles with the salt and
sprinkle over the kale before baking.

sweet kale chips
Omit the salt, mix together 1 teaspoon superfine sugar and 1 teaspoon
cinnamon and sprinkle over instead of the salt.

cumin & coriander
Dry fry 1 teaspoon cumin seeds and 1 teaspoon coriander seeds for
2 minutes until their aroma is released. Crush in a pestle and mortar, mix
with the salt and sprinkle over the kale before baking.

soy sauce
Sprinkle with a little dark soy sauce just before serving or serve with a bowl
of soy sauce as a dip.

variations

aduki bean dip

see base recipe page 52

spicy aduki & pomegranate dip
Omit the tahini and sesame seeds, add 1 roasted red bell pepper, skin removed, 1 finely chopped red chile and 1 teaspoon pomegranate molasses. Serve with a few fresh pomegranate seeds sprinkled on top.

smoky aduki bean dip
Make as above adding 2 teaspoons smoked chipotle paste.

indian aduki bean dip
Omit the tahini and sesame seeds, add 1 teaspoon ground cumin, 1/2 teaspoon ground turmeric, 3/4 inch grated fresh gingerroot and an extra clove of garlic, crushed, add more lemon juice if a little thick.

black bean dip
Replace the aduki beans with black beans, the lemon with lime juice and add 1 tablespoon chopped fresh cilantro at the end to create color and extra flavor.

sprouted sunflower seeds hummus

see base recipe page 53

roasted red bell pepper sunflower seeds hummus

Add 2 roasted red bell peppers either from a jar or roasted in the oven and skin removed with the rest of the ingredients.

spicy sunflower seeds hummus

Add either 1 fresh red chile, finely diced or 1/4 teaspoon hot chili powder.

rose harissa sunflower seeds hummus

Replace the garam masala with 1/2 teaspoon ground cinnamon, 1 teaspoon sweet paprika and 1 teaspoon rose harissa, replace the lime juice with lemon juice.

pumpkin hummus

Replace the sunflower seeds with pumpkin seeds, add 1 cup chopped fresh raw pumpkin and puree as in main recipe.

variations

whole-grain pita chips

see base recipe page 54

soy pita chips
Mix 2 tablespoons dark soy sauce with a tablespoon of olive or sesame oil, brush over the pita ovals once you have split them but before cutting into triangles. Bake as in main recipe.

cumin & coriander pita chips
Roughly grind 1 teaspoon cumin seeds and 1 teaspoon coriander seeds in a pestle and mortar, sprinkle over the pita chips before baking.

moroccan pita chips
Mix together 1 teaspoon sweet paprika, 1 teaspoon sea salt, pinch of sugar, 1/2 teaspoon ground cinnamon, 1/2 teaspoon ground cumin, 1/2 teaspoon ground coriander and a pinch of chili powder, sprinkle over the pita triangles before baking.

italian pita chips
Mix together 1 tablespoon extra virgin olive oil, 1 teaspoon dried oregano, 1 teaspoon garlic salt, 1/2 teaspoon freshly ground black pepper, brush over the pita. Cut the pita ovals into triangles and bake.

variations

tapenade

see base recipe page 55

sun-dried tomato tapenade
Add 6 sun-dried tomatoes, drained of oil and patted dry, and use the oil in the place of the extra virgin olive oil to add more flavor.

green olive & fresh cilantro tapenade
Replace the black olives with green olives and add 2 tablespoons chopped fresh cilantro.

green olive & feta cheese tapenade
Replace the black olives with green olives, puree, transfer to a serving bowl and stir in 1/2 cup finely crumbled feta.

with anchovies & capers
Add 6 anchovy fillets, drained and patted dry, and 1/2 tablespoon rinsed capers.

tapenade twists
Roll out a sheet of flaky pastry, spread with a thin layer of tapenade, cut into strips 3/4 inch-wide and twist the strips. Transfer to a greased cookie sheet and bake in a hot oven for 8–12 minutes until golden brown and crispy.

variations

guacamole

see base recipe page 56

chunky with fresh chile
Finely dice the avocado, stir in the lime juice, a few finely chopped cherry tomatoes and 1 finely chopped, deseeded red chile.

smoky guacamole
Omit the chili powder and add 1 teaspoon chipotle paste.

with pomegranates and cilantro
Make as before sprinkling over 1 tablespoon finely chopped fresh cilantro and 1 tablespoon fresh pomegranate seeds to serve.

with Greek yogurt
Stir in 1 tablespoon Greek yogurt and 2 chopped shallots, sauteed until soft and golden brown in a little olive oil. Serve with a sprinkling of dry roasted cumin seeds.

cucumber tarts with smoked oysters & cream cheese

see base recipe page 57

creamy crab filling
Replace the smoked oysters with 6 ounces of crab meat.

smoked mackerel filling
Replace the smoked oysters with two smoked mackerel fillets.

smoked salmon & cream cheese filling
Omit the smoked oysters, mix the cream cheese with the lemon juice and seasoning, spoon into the cucumber tarts, and top with a little smoked salmon and fresh dill.

spicy avocado prawn filling
Replace the smoked oysters and cream cheese with 2 ripe avocados, flesh scooped out and mashed with 1 fresh red chile, finely chopped and 1 tablespoon fresh cilantro, chopped. Replace the lemon juice with lime juice and mix everything together. Place teaspoonfuls on the cucumber tarts and top with a small prawn.

variations

spicy cashew nuts

see base recipe page 58

salt & pepper cashews

Omit the cumin seeds, coriander seeds, chili flakes and sugar, add
1 teaspoon freshly ground black pepper and proceed with main recipe.

mixed nuts

Replace the cashews with 2 cups mixed nuts such as pecans, hazelnuts,
Brazil nuts, and macadamia nuts.

spicy soy cashew nuts

Replace the oil with 1 teaspoon sesame oil. Omit the cumin seeds, coriander
seeds, and sugar, add 1 teaspoon five spice powder, 2 teaspoons dark soy
sauce and preheat the oven to 350°F (180°C). Pour the oil, spices and soy
sauce over the cashews, spread the nuts onto a cookie sheet and bake for
10-15 minutes until they begin to darken. Cool and serve.

sweet cinnamon cashews

Omit the spices and sugar, mix together the sunflower oil with 1 teaspoon
ground cinnamon, and 2 tablespoons agave or honey. Pour over the nuts,
spread over a cookie sheet and bake at 350°F (180°C) for 10-15 minutes.
Cool completely before serving.

cheewra

see base recipe page 61

nut-free version

Omit the cashew nuts and peanuts, replace with 6 tablespoons puffed rice and 3 tablespoons pumpkin seeds, heated in a little oil until popped, plus 3 tablespoons sesame seeds.

sweet version

Omit the turmeric and black pepper, increase the cinnamon to 1 teaspoon and reduce the salt to a large pinch. Add 1/3 cup dark chocolate chips once the mixture has cooled.

spicy version

Make as before adding 1/2 teaspoon crushed chiles to the mixture along with the salt and sugar.

with kale chips

Proceed with main recipe, adding a portion of kale chips (see page 51) once cooled.

soups

This chapter is brimming with super soups, packed with goodness for any lunch, appetizer, or light main course.

gazpacho

see variations page 87

This chilled tomato soup is full of antioxidants and loses very little of the nutrients in the vegetables as they're raw. Ideal on a warm summer day.

2 x 14-oz. cans chopped tomatoes
1 red onion, diced
1 red bell pepper, deseeded and diced
1 orange bell pepper, deseeded and diced
1/2 cucumber, seeds removed and diced
1 tbsp. balsamic vinegar, plus extra to serve

juice of 1 lemon
1 tsp. coriander seeds
1 tsp. mixed peppercorns
extra virgin olive oil, to serve
fresh basil leaves, to serve

Blend the tomatoes and onion in a blender or food processor until smooth.

Add half the bell peppers and 2/3 of the cucumber along with the balsamic vinegar and lemon juice and blend again until mostly smooth.

Pound the coriander seeds and peppercorns in a pestle and mortar until roughly ground, then stir into the tomato base. Chill until ready to serve.

To serve, scatter over the remaining chopped bell peppers and cucumber, and drizzle over a little balsamic vinegar and a splash of extra virgin olive oil. You could also scatter over a few basil leaves to finish.

Serves 4–6

roasted red bell pepper soup

see variations page 88

Deeply red, full of antioxidants and cancer-protecting lycopene, this soup feels like it's doing you good with each mouthful.

5 red bell peppers
6 large, ripe tomatoes, halved
2 red onions, skinned and quartered
2 garlic cloves, peeled
1 tbsp. extra virgin olive oil
1 tbsp. balsamic vinegar

1 tsp. sugar
pinch sea salt
pinch black pepper
1 tbsp. fresh basil, chopped
4 cups vegetable broth
whole-grain bread, to serve

Preheat the oven to 425°F (220°C).

Place the bell peppers, tomatoes, onions and garlic in a roasting pan, drizzle with the olive oil and balsamic vinegar, sugar and a good pinch of sea salt and freshly ground black pepper.

Sprinkle the basil over the vegetables and roast for 30–40 minutes until they are starting to char at the edges.

Remove the roasting pan from the oven, and carefully tip the contents into a large saucepan, add the broth and bring to a boil. Simmer gently for 20 minutes, transfer to a blender to liquidize or use an immersion blender, check the seasoning and serve with crusty whole-grain bread.

Serves 4

roasted tomato soup

see variations page 89

Tomato soup is the ultimate comfort food, and this version roasts the tomatoes to obtain the best flavor and adds basil, garlic, and red onion to boost your immunity.

2 lb. 3 oz. tomatoes, skinned and halved
2 garlic heads, tops chopped off
2 tbsp. olive oil plus extra
1 tbsp. balsamic vinegar
bunch of fresh basil
2 red onions, diced

2 carrots, diced
2 tbsp. tomato paste
4 cups vegetable broth
sea salt and freshly ground black pepper
extra virgin olive oil, to serve

Preheat the oven to 400°F (200°C). Lay the tomatoes, cut side-up in a deep roasting pan, and repeat with the garlic heads. Drizzle with olive oil then balsamic vinegar. Tear off enough basil leaves for the number of tomato halves, coat the leaves in oil and lay one leaf on each tomato half. Tear the remaining basil leaves and set aside. Sprinkle with sea salt and freshly ground black pepper and roast for 40–50 minutes until the edges of the tomatoes are charred at the edges and starting to caramelize.

In a separate saucepan, sauté the onion until softened, add the carrot and cook for another 5 minutes. Add the tomato paste, broth, and half the remaining basil leaves and bring to a simmer. Remove the roasting pan from the oven, squeeze the garlic cloves out of the heads into the saucepan and scrape with the roasted tomatoes and juices. Simmer for 20–25 minutes. Season to taste and blend to a smooth puree in a food processor or using an immersion blender. Serve with a drizzle of oil and torn basil.

Serves 4

pumpkin soup

see variations page 90

Use small, culinary pumpkins to make soup, not the ones that you would carve into lanterns. Butternut squash works as well.

1 pumpkin (about 2 lb. 10 oz.)
1 tbsp. olive oil
1 1/2 tbsp. butter
1 red onion, diced
2 carrots, diced

3 cups vegetable broth
1 cup milk
freshy grated nutmeg
salt and freshly ground black pepper
sour cream and warm bread, to serve

Preheat the oven to 350°F (180°C). Cut the pumpkin in half and remove the seeds. Cut each half into 4 again and brush with half the olive oil. Season with salt and pepper and put flesh-side-down in the roasting pan. Roast for 25 minutes until soft and golden brown.

Melt the butter in a large saucepan, add the onion and carrots, cook over a gentle heat for about 20 minutes, until soft and the onion is translucent. Remove the pumpkin from the oven, set aside to cool. Add the broth and milk to the vegetables and gently bring to a simmer, add the freshly grated nutmeg.

Remove the pumpkin skin and cut the flesh into chunks. Add to the saucepan, bring back to a simmer and cook for 15 minutes. Transfer to a liquidizer or use an immersion blender and puree until smooth. Check the seasoning and serve hot with a swirl of sour cream and warm bread.

Serves 4

green goodness soup

see variations page 91

So called as it's packed full of veggie goodness.

2 tbsp. olive oil
2 leeks, chopped
4 garlic cloves, thinly sliced
4 cups vegetable broth
1 bunch broccoli, cut into florets
1 zucchini, diced

1/2 cup peas
3 cups spinach
3 cups kale (stalks removed, chopped)
1 tsp. matcha green tea powder
juice of 2 lemons
sea salt and freshly ground black pepper

In a large saucepan, add the oil and sauté the chopped leeks for 5 minutes until soft, add the garlic and sauté for another 2 minutes.

Pour in the broth and bring to a boil. Reduce to a simmer and add the broccoli and diced zucchini, cook for 3–4 minutes. Add the peas, spinach, chopped kale, matcha, and lemon juice and simmer for 2–3 minutes until the spinach and kale have wilted. Blend to a smooth puree in a food processor or using an immersion blender.

Taste, adjust seasoning if necessary, and serve.

Serves 2

beet soup

see variations page 92

The rich color of this soup is a sign of its high nutrient value.

1 lb. ripe tomatoes
1 lb. raw beets, peeled and chopped
1 garlic clove, finely chopped
1 onion, finely chopped
2 tbsp. sunflower oil

1 tsp. dried thyme
2 cups, plus 1 tbsp. beef or vegetable broth
sea salt and freshly ground black pepper
sour cream and feta cheese, to serve

Preheat the oven to 400°F (200°C).

Halve the tomatoes and lay on a cookie sheet along with the beets, garlic, and onions. Drizzle with oil, sprinkle with thyme and roast for 25–30 minutes until soft, turning half-way through.

Remove the skins from the tomatoes and transfer to a large saucepan. Add the broth and simmer over a low heat for 10–15 minutes until the beets are soft. Season to taste.

Use an immersion blender and puree until smooth. Serve with a drizzle of sour cream and sprinkling of feta cheese.

Serves 4

watercress soup

see variations page 93

This soup is light, satisfying, and super good for you.

1 tbsp. olive oil
1 onion, chopped
1 leek, diced
2 medium potatoes, peeled and diced
4 cups chicken or vegetable broth
1 cup watercress, plus extra to serve

1/2 cup, plus 2 tbsp. milk or almond/soy milk
pinch freshly grated nutmeg
juice of 1 lemon
sea salt and freshly ground black pepper
crème fraiche, to serve
crusty seeded bread, to serve

Heat the oil in a large saucepan, add the onion and leek and cook over a low heat for around 10 minutes until softened but not browned. Stir in the potatoes and broth and bring to a boil. Cover and simmer for 10–15 minutes until the potato is tender.

Stir in the watercress (reserving a sprig for serving), cover and cook for 5 minutes. Puree with an immersion blender or transfer to a blender until smooth.

Return the soup to the saucepan and add the milk, nutmeg and lemon juice, season and gently reheat (do not allow the soup to boil once the milk has been added).

Serve hot with a swirl of crème fraiche, a sprig of watercress and some crusty seeded bread.

Serves 4

carrot & cilantro soup

see variations page 94

This easy soup is packed with goodness, serve with seeded or whole-grain bread.

1 tbsp. sunflower oil
1 onion, chopped
1 tsp. ground coriander
8 medium carrots, peeled and chopped

5 cups vegetable broth
sea salt and freshly ground black pepper
handful of fresh cilantro, finely chopped

Heat the oil in a large skillet, add the onion and fry over a low heat for 5–10 minutes until translucent and soft rather than browned. Add the ground coriander and fry for 1–2 minutes until fragrant.

Add the carrots, cover, and allow the vegetables to cook gently for 5–10 minutes until the carrots soften. Add the broth, bring to a boil, cover, reduce the heat, and simmer for 15–20 minutes until the carrots are tender.

Puree the soup in a food processor or with an immersion blender. Taste and adjust the seasoning if required, serve with a sprinkling of fresh cilantro.

Serves 4

souper noodles

see variations page 95

Super-quick, super-healthy, the ultimate fast superfood.

4 cups vegetable broth
1-in. fresh gingerroot, grated
1 garlic clove, very finely sliced
1/2 cup noodles, such as buckwheat, soba,
    low-carb, egg, etc
4 scallions, finely sliced
4 mushrooms, finely sliced

1 bok choy, finely shredded
1/4 cup sugar snap peas, halved
4 baby sweet corn, halved
1 tbsp. miso paste
2 tsp. dark soy sauce
1 fresh red chile, finely sliced
handful of fresh cilantro, chopped

In a large saucepan bring the vegetable broth to a boil. Add the ginger and garlic and keep just below a simmer for 10 minutes, letting the flavors develop.

Add the noodles and the rest of the ingredients except the miso paste, soy sauce and chile and simmer for 2–3 minutes to heat through. Split the miso paste between two bowls, pour over some of the broth and stir to dissolve the miso paste. Add the soy sauce and mix.

Ladle the remaining soup into the bowls, sprinkle the chile and fresh cilantro on top and serve.

Serves 2

variations

gazpacho

see base recipe page 75

with pesto
Proceed with main recipe and serve with a spoonful of pesto on top of the chopped cucumber and bell peppers.

with cucumber salsa
Add all the bell peppers to the tomato base and puree, dice the remaining cucumber and mix with 4 skinned, deseeded, diced tomatoes, 1 deseeded, finely diced fresh red chile, and a handful of chopped fresh basil leaves. Spoon onto the chilled soup to serve.

with chunky guacamole
Add all the bell peppers and cucumber to the tomato base and puree. Omit the basil leaves and spoon guacamole (see page 56) onto the chilled soup to serve.

fresh tomato gazpacho
If you can source ripe tomatoes, they must be ripe and smell fabulous, then omit one of the tins of tomatoes and replace with 5 chopped ripe tomatoes.

variations

roasted red bell pepper soup

see base recipe page 76

with lima beans & oregano
Proceed with main recipe, replacing the fresh basil with freshly chopped oregano. To serve, warm through 2 cups cooked lima beans and serve in the center of the soup with a little chopped oregano sprinkled over.

with wild rice & spirulina
Cook just under 1/2 cup wild rice, mix with 1 teaspoon spirulina powder, and a good pinch of cajun season. Serve on top of the soup; it will fall in and settle in a pile at the base.

with spelt macaroni
Cook 1 cup spelt or whole-grain macaroni, share it between the bowls, pour over the soup and finish with freshly grated parmesan for a more substantial soup.

roasted tomato soup

see base recipe page 78

beany tomato soup
Drain and rinse a 14-ounce can of borlotti beans or black-eye peas, stir into the soup after pureeing and reheat for 5 minutes to make sure the beans are hot.

with lentils, ginger & turmeric
Add 1/2 cup red lentils to the soup when adding the roasted tomatoes, along with 2 inches fresh gingerroot, grated and 1 teaspoon ground turmeric.

with smoked paprika & chili
For a Moroccan feel, replace the basil with fresh oregano and add 2 teaspoons sweet paprika and 1 teaspoon hot chili powder.

with cheesy croutons
Cut 4 slices of whole-grain, sourdough, or spelt bread, toast, drizzle with a little olive oil and rub over a garlic clove. Sprinkle with grated parmesan and toast until the cheese melts. Serve on the side with the soup.

variations

pumpkin soup

see base recipe page 79

with pumpkin seed popkins
Popkins are pumpkin seeds that have been "popped" like popcorn. Proceed with main recipe and in a small saucepan heat 1 tablespoon sunflower oil. Add sufficient pumpkin seeds to cover the bottom of the saucepan in one layer, cover with a lid and shake the saucepan until you hear popping sounds. Once the popping subsides, carefully remove the lid, drain on paper towels and sprinkle with a little salt. Spoon into the center of each bowl of soup. They're delicious served as nibbles.

with coriander seeds
Omit the nutmeg and replace with 2 teaspoons coriander seeds, dry-fried and roughly ground in a pestle and mortar. Sprinkle over 1 tablespoon finely chopped fresh cilantro before serving.

curried pumpkin soup with rice
This turns the soup into a more substantial meal. Replace the nutmeg with 1–2 teaspoons madras curry powder, depending on how hot you like your soup. Cook 1/2 cup brown basmati rice. After pureeing the soup stir in the rice and heat through. Sprinkle over a little finely chopped fresh cilantro and serve.

green goodness soup

see base recipe page 81

with mint
Omit the matcha and add 1 tablespoon chopped fresh mint with the spinach.

with pesto & pine nuts
Add 1 teaspoon pesto just before serving, sprinkle with pine nuts.

with beans
Stir in a 14-ounce can of drained and rinsed cannellini beans with the spinach.

with potatoes for a thicker soup
Cook 2 medium peeled and diced potatoes in the broth for 10 minutes before adding the leeks. Blend the soup to a puree before serving.

variations

beet soup

see base recipe page 82

borscht
Omit the tomatoes, grate the beet and add 2 grated carrots and 2 medium potatoes, peeled and cubed. Sweat all the vegetables over a low heat for 5-10 minutes, transfer to a saucepan, add 3 tablespoons tomato puree and 1 tablespoon red wine vinegar. Cook for 20-25 minutes until all the vegetables are tender. Serve with a swirl of sour cream.

with goat cheese croutons
Proceed with main recipe and cut 4 slices of baguette. Toast one side, and on the untoasted side spread goat cheese and toast under a broiler, lay on top of the soup just before serving.

spicy beet soup
Proceed with main recipe, adding 2 chopped fresh red chiles at the same time as the broth.

with crème fraiche & goat cheese
Proceed with the main recipe, replacing the sour cream and feta with crème fraiche and goat cheese.

watercress soup

see base recipe page 84

with peas
Add 1 1/2 cups fresh or frozen peas to the mixture at the same time as the watercress, proceed with main recipe.

with cooked chicken
Add 4 ounces cooked, shredded chicken to the soup at the same time as the watercress, proceed with main recipe.

with spinach
Add 5 cups spinach to the soup at the same time as the watercress, proceed with main recipe.

variations

carrot & cilantro soup

see base recipe page 85

carrot & orange soup
Omit the ground coriander and fresh cilantro. Add the grated zest and juice of two oranges at the same time as the broth, reduce the broth to 4 cups. Garnish with sprigs of fresh mint.

carrot, orange & ginger soup
Proceed with the recipe for carrot & orange soup above, and add 4 inches freshly grated gingerroot at the same time as the orange. Serve with a swirl of natural yogurt and some chopped chives.

carrot, lentil & spinach soup
Add 1 cup red lentils at the same time as the broth, add 5 cups fresh, chopped spinach 5 minutes before the end of the cooking time along with the juice of 1 lime.

curried carrot soup
Add 1 teaspoon ground cumin and 1 teaspoon Madras curry powder at the same time as the ground coriander.

variations

souper noodles

see base recipe page 86

chicken souper noodles
Add 1 thinly sliced chicken breast to the vegetable broth with the ginger and garlic, proceed with main recipe.

green souper noodles
Omit the mushrooms and sweet corn, replace with a handful of fresh or frozen peas, 1 thinly sliced zucchini and 4 sliced asparagus spears.

tofu souper noodles
Add 1 cup silken tofu, cubed, with the vegetables.

brown rice soup
Replace the noodles with 1/4 cup cooked whole-grain rice.

salads

Salads are probably the most obvious dishes that

come to mind when we think about superfoods.

Here is a delicious selection that the whole family

will enjoy.

quinoa tabbouleh

see variations page 115

A superfood version of classic tabbouleh using quinoa in place of bulgar wheat, delicious on its own in a whole-grain flatbread with a drizzle of yogurt or served with a selection of other salads or grilled meat.

1 cup quinoa
zest and juice of 2 lemons
1 garlic clove, finely chopped
1/4 cup extra virgin olive oil
1 cup cherry tomatoes, chopped

small bunch mint, chopped
small bunch flat leaf parsley, chopped
4 scallions, finely sliced
1 small cucumber, chopped
1/2 cup pomegranate seeds

Rinse the quinoa in cold water. Cook the quinoa in 2 cups water for 15–20 minutes until tender and the water has been absorbed. Rinse in cold water and let cool.

Make up the dressing by lightly whisking together the lemon zest and juice, garlic and olive oil. Pour this over the cooled quinoa and stir gently to mix.

Add the chopped tomatoes, herbs, scallions, cucumber and pomegranate seeds, and gently stir to mix. Chill and bring to room temperature to serve.

Serves 3–4

superfood salad

see variations page 116

This can be adapted to suit whatever you have in your refrigerator. It's super-healthy, gluten-free, and high in protein with the use of quinoa, just try to include as many different colored vegetables as you can.

1 large sweet potato or small butternut squash, peeled and diced
1 raw beet, peeled and diced
2 red onions, peeled and cut into sixths
2 bell peppers, red, yellow, or orange, stalk removed and cut into eighths
olive oil spray
1 cup quinoa
2 1/2 cups, plus 1 tbsp. vegetable or chicken broth

small bunch fresh mint leaves, chopped
small bunch fresh cilantro, chopped
zest and juice of 1 lemon
salad leaves, including baby spinach
1/2 cup sprouted seeds or beans, cooked and chilled, if required
seeds of 1 pomegranate
sea salt and freshly ground black pepper
dressing made from 2 tbsp. extra virgin olive oil and the juice of 1 lemon

Preheat the oven to 400°F (200°C).

Place the diced sweet potato, beet, onions, and sliced bell pepper on a greased, non-stick cookie sheet and spray with olive oil. Season and roast for 20–25 minutes until just starting to catch at the edges. Remove from the oven and let cool. Place the quinoa in a saucepan, pour over the broth, bring to a simmer and cook for 15 minutes to allow the quinoa to soak up the broth. Then turn off the heat, fork through, and let cool.

Once the quinoa and vegetables have cooled stir the mint and fresh cilantro into the quinoa along with the lemon zest and juice.

To assemble the salad, gently stir the roasted vegetables into the quinoa, lay the salad leaves in a bowl, toss over the roasted root vegetables, scatter over the sprouted seeds and pomegranate seeds.

To make the dressing, whisk the extra virgin olive oil with the lemon juice, drizzle over the salad and serve.

This will keep for up to 3 days in the refrigerator without the dressing. Make the dressing up and drizzle over the salad just before serving each time. It's also easy to pack in a plastic container to take to work with you.

Serves 4

giant couscous salad with grilled peaches & feta

see variations page 117

A deliciously refreshing salad or side dish which goes well with broiled chicken or lamb. Giant couscous is known as moghrabiah and originates in the Middle East. The combination of the baby spinach, arugula, cheese, and fruit works well and gives you an iron and calcium boost.

1 cup giant whole-grain couscous
2 tbsp. olive oil, plus extra to toast
4 ripe peaches or nectarines
2 tsp. rose harissa
juice of 1 lemon

mixture of baby spinach and arugula leaves
1/2 cup feta, crumbled
mint leaves, to serve
1/3 cup toasted pine nuts

Toast the couscous in a skillet with a little oil, shaking frequently, until it becomes golden brown. Add sufficient water, gradually, until the couscous has swelled and is soft. This should take around 20 minutes, keep adding water little by little until it has been absorbed.

Heat a grill pan for around 5 minutes until smoking hot. Skin the peaches; if they are ripe these should easily slip off. If they are difficult to remove, plunge them into a bowl of boiling water and leave for 1–2 minutes, drain, refresh under cold water so they are cool enough to handle and slip off the skins. Halve them, remove the pit and cut each half into 4 wedges.

Mix some of the rose harissa with the olive oil and paint each side of the peaches.

Cook on the grill for a few minutes until they have lovely charred lines, turn over and repeat with the other side.

Mix the remaining olive oil and harissa with the lemon juice, and drizzle over the spinach and arugula leaves, toss to coat the leaves. Add the cooked giant couscous and gently mix. Arrange the grilled peaches on top, sprinkle with crumbled feta and scatter with some torn mint leaves and a few toasted pine nuts.

Serves 4

warm chicken salad with matcha pesto dressing

see variations page 118

Not quite as "superfood" as my superfood salad but pretty crammed with delicious goodness all the same. Matcha green tea powder is a concentrated form of green tea and is high in antioxidants. It blends really well with the pesto.

4 skinless, boneless chicken breasts
extra virgin olive oil
1 cup broccolini tips
mixed salad leaves, including baby spinach
1 cup cherry tomatoes, halved
parmesan shavings
1/3 cup pine nuts
sea salt and freshly ground black pepper

Dressing:
1 tbsp. fresh pesto
1 tbsp. extra virgin olive oil
1/2 tsp. matcha green tea powder
juice and zest of 1 lemon

Heat a grill pan until it's very hot. Slice the chicken and brush with olive oil and season. Cook on the grill pan until the slices have lovely grill lines and are thoroughly cooked through.

Meanwhile, steam the broccolini tips for 3–4 minutes until just tender, then immediately refresh in ice water to cool.

Mix the dressing by whisking together the pesto, olive oil, matcha powder, lemon juice and zest. Assemble the salad with the salad leaves, broccolini tips, and cherry tomato halves. Toss over the dressing, top with the warm chicken slices and scatter over the parmesan shavings and pine nuts. Serve while still warm.

Serves 4

indian carrot salad

see variations page 119

Quick and easy to prepare but bursting with flavor, lovely served with Kashmiri curry, with dhal, or with bean burgers.

2 tbsp. sunflower oil
1 tbsp. black mustard seeds
4 carrots, peeled and grated
1 tbsp. whole sesame seeds
large pinch sea salt
juice of 1 lemon

Heat the oil in a small skillet, add the mustard seeds, and as soon as they begin to pop, remove from the heat and toss over the grated carrots. Add the sesame seeds and salt and mix well, drizzle over the lemon juice, mix one last time and serve.

Serves 4

greek beans

see variations page 120

Wonderful served as a side dish or added to a bowlful of salad leaves and dressed with some classic olive oil dressing. Serve the beans at room temperature. They are best made the day before to allow the flavor to develop.

2 x 14-oz. cans lima beans
2 tbsp. Greek extra virgin olive oil, plus extra
    for drizzling
1 large onion, finely chopped
2 garlic cloves, finely chopped
14-oz. can chopped tomatoes or
    tomato passata

1 tbsp. tomato paste
1 tsp. dried oregano
1 tbsp. fresh flat leaf parsley, finely chopped,
    plus extra for serving
1 tbsp. fresh mint, finely chopped, plus extra
    for serving
sea salt and freshly ground black pepper

Drain and thoroughly rinse the beans, set aside.

Heat the oil and fry the onion and garlic over a low heat for around 10 minutes until translucent and soft but not browned. Add the tomatoes or passata, tomato paste, and the beans. Season, add the oregano, and simmer for 10–15 minutes until the tomato has reduced to a thick sauce.

Remove from the heat, stir in the fresh herbs, and let cool. Refrigerate until ready to serve. Serve with a drizzle of olive oil and a few more chopped fresh herbs.

Serves 4

classic vinaigrette dressing

see variations page 121

Make in a clean screw top jar and keep in your refrigerator for up to 1 week for instant salad dressing with pure ingredients that taste fabulous.

juice of 2 lemons
extra virgin olive oil (around 4 tbsp.)
pinch sea salt
1 garlic clove, crushed whole*

*To crush a whole garlic clove, remove the skin and use the flat side of a knife over the top of the garlic, push down until the clove "pops" and splits but still remains intact.

Put the lemon juice in a screw top jar, add the same amount of extra virgin olive oil, a pinch of sea salt and pop the whole crushed garlic clove in too. Secure the lid and give it a good shake. Pour over salad leaves and toss the leaves to cover.

Keep topping up the dressing with the same quantity of lemon juice and olive oil, leaving the garlic clove as it is for a couple of weeks before replacing it.

Serves 2–3

gado gado

see variations page 122

This Indonesian salad with noodles is a delicious treat.

1/2 cup snow peas
1/2 cup green beans, halved
1 cup bean sprouts
1 orange or red bell pepper,
    sliced
1/2 cucumber, quartered,
    seeds removed and cut
    into matchsticks
zest and juice of 2 limes

handful of fresh cilantro,
    chopped
2 cups egg noodles
2 tbsp. peanut butter
1 garlic clove, crushed
1 red chile, deseeded and
    finely chopped
1 tsp. coconut sugar or agave
    syrup

1 tsp. fish sauce or soy sauce
1/2 cup coconut cream
little gem lettuce leaves
sea salt and freshly ground
    black pepper

Blanch and refresh the snow peas, green beans, and bean sprouts. Mix the blanched vegetables with the bell pepper and cucumber, stir in the zest and juice of 1 lime and the fresh cilantro. Set aside. Cook the noodles per the instructions on the package, refresh in iced water and set aside.

Mix together the peanut butter, garlic, red chile, coconut sugar, fish sauce, and coconut cream. Check the seasoning. Heat a dry skillet, add the peanuts and lightly toast until golden brown, chop roughly. Pile the vegetables onto the little gem lettuce leaves, stir a tablespoon of the peanut sauce into the noodles and pile the noodles next to the lettuce and drizzle peanut sauce over the vegetables.

Serves 4

nicoise salad

see variations page 123

The tuna, egg, and raw vegetables in this salad make it a super-easy superfood lunch. If you have a mandolin this is fabulous for thinly slicing the vegetables.

3 cups watercress
7 cups baby spinach
3 cups romaine lettuce or baby leaves
4 ripe tomatoes, chopped
1/2 small cucumber, chopped
2 red bell peppers, chopped
1 red onion, thinly sliced
8 radishes, thinly sliced
1 bunch asparagus, trimmed, steamed and
    cooled
1 cup green beans, steamed, cooled and halved
4 hard boiled eggs, peeled and quartered

chopped fresh parsley
10 1/2-oz. can sustainably caught tuna in
    spring water, drained
1/3 cup black olives, pitted

Dressing:
juice of 1 lemon
1/2 tsp. dijon mustard
2 garlic cloves, crushed
3 tbsp. extra virgin olive oil
large pinch sea salt

Combine all the salad ingredients in a large bowl.

Make the dressing by putting the lemon juice, mustard, garlic, and olive oil into a clean screw top jar, season, replace the lid, and shake well until it becomes creamy. Pour over the salad and serve.

Serves 4

chermoula chicken salad

see variations page 124

Chermoula is a marinade used in North African cooking, frequently with fish, in this case with chicken. It is light and fragrant and helps the chicken keep moist.

4 boneless skinless chicken breasts
1/2 tsp. coriander seeds
1/2 tsp. cumin seeds
1 small red onion, peeled and roughly chopped
2 garlic cloves, peeled and sliced
2 fresh red chiles
1 tbsp. fresh mint leaves, chopped
pinch sea salt
extra virgin olive oil
juice and zest of 2 lemons

Sauce:
juice of 2 lemons
juice of 1 pink grapefruit
1 tbsp. maple syrup

Garden salad:
Bag of baby salad leaves or mixture of baby
    spinach, arugula, pea shoots, etc
1/3 cup fresh garden peas
1 zucchini, cut into ribbons with a vegetable
    peeler

Flatten each chicken breast using a freezer bag and rolling pin or tenderizer. Dry-fry the coriander and cumin seeds in a skillet until fragrant, be careful not to burn. Transfer to a pestle and mortar and pound to a powder.

Put the red onion, garlic, chiles, mint, salt, 4–5 tablespoons olive oil, and the lemon juice and zest in a small food processor and blend. Tip into a bowl, add the chicken breasts and spice powder and rub the oil and herbs into the chicken, making sure they are thoroughly covered. Cover with plastic wrap and marinate in the refrigerator for at least 4 hours.

When ready to cook, heat a grill pan, add a little oil if needed and cook the chicken, reserving the marinade.

To make the citrus sauce, put the marinade in a small saucepan along with the lemon juice, grapefruit juice, and maple syrup, bring to a boil and reduce to a thick sauce.

To make the salad, arrange the leaves, fresh peas, and zucchini ribbons in a bowl, drizzle with a little olive oil, sprinkle over a little salt and gently stir to mix. You don't want much dressing as there will be plenty of sauce from the marinade. Serve the chicken with the citrus sauce on the side.

Serves 4

super coleslaw

see variations page 125

Super coleslaw has rainbow colors, bursts with flavor and is lower in fat than your standard coleslaw.

1 apple
1 carrot
1/2 red cabbage
3/4 cup plain yogurt

2 tsp. black mustard seeds
juice of 1 lemon or lime
sea salt and freshly ground black pepper

Peel and grate the apple and carrot, finely slice the cabbage. If you have a mandolin this is perfect for very fine slicing.

Mix together the yogurt, mustard seeds, and lemon or lime juice. Pour over the vegetables and gently mix, season to taste, and serve.

Serves 4

quinoa tabbouleh

see base recipe page 97

with couscous
Replace the quinoa with the same quantity of couscous. Place the couscous in a heat proof bowl and cover with boiling water, cover the bowl with a clean towel and leave for 5 minutes, fluff up the couscous and let cool.

with toasted seeds
Proceed with main recipe and in a dry skillet fry 2/3 cup mixed sunflower, pumpkin, chia and sesame seeds until fragrant. Sprinkle over the tabbouleh just before serving.

with sprouted seeds
Proceed with main recipe and stir in 2/3 cup sprouted seeds at the same time as the pomegranate seeds.

harissa
For a spicy version proceed with main recipe, adding 1 teaspoon rose harissa to the lemon juice and mix with the dressing.

variations

superfood salad

see base recipe page 98

even more super superfood salad
Steam 1/2 cup snow peas and 1/4 cup edamame beans for 3 minutes, refresh in cold water and add to the salad.

superfood salad with feta cheese
Increase the protein by scattering over 1/2 cup feta cheese just before serving.

superfood salad with sun-dried tomatoes & olives
Add 1 tablespoon drained, chopped sun-dried tomatoes to the quinoa once cooked and add 1 tablespoon sun-dried tomato and olive tapenade to the dressing.

superfood salad with giant couscous & harissa
Omit the quinoa, fry 1 cup giant whole-grain couscous in a little olive oil until lightly browned. Add broth a little at a time, stirring until the couscous soaks up the liquid, keep adding until the couscous is al dente. Stir in 1 tablespoon rose harissa and proceed with main recipe.

giant couscous salad with grilled peaches & feta

see base recipe page 100

with watermelon
Replace the peaches with 2 1/2 cups fresh, cubed watermelon, do not cook it.

griddled eggplant, feta & mint
Replace the peaches with 2 eggplants, finely sliced and grilled in batches.

with broiled lamb
Cube 7 ounces lamb leg steaks and broil them quickly so they are charred on the edges but still tender in the middle. Mix with the peaches and rest of the salad.

harissa roast bell peppers & goat cheese
Replace the peaches with 1 red, 1 orange and 1 yellow bell pepper. Remove the stalks and seeds and cut into 8 thick strips, brush with the oil and harissa and roast in a hot oven for 20–25 minutes until slightly charred at the edges. Mix with the couscous and leaves as in main recipe. Replace the feta with crumbled goat cheese.

variations

warm chicken salad with matcha pesto dressing

see base recipe page 103

with sun-dried tomato & olive dressing
Replace the pesto with 1 tablespoon sun-dried tomato and black olive tapenade. Omit the matcha.

veggie version
Omit the chicken, roast 1 eggplant, 1 zucchini and 2 red bell peppers for 20–25 minutes in a hot oven. Serve with the matcha pesto dressing.

orange & walnut
Replace the pine nuts with 1/3 cup walnuts, chopped and dry-fried until just starting to color. Replace the lemon juice and zest with orange juice and zest. Omit the matcha.

green bean & hazelnut
Add 1/2 cup chopped, steamed, and cooled green beans, omit the parmesan, replace the pine nuts with 1/3 cup chopped roasted hazelnuts and replace the dressing with 1 tablespoon hazelnut oil and the zest and juice of 1 orange. Sprinkle with a handful of chopped hazelnuts, omit the matcha.

indian carrot salad

see base recipe page 104

thai carrot salad
Replace the sesame seeds with 2 tablespoons chopped, roasted peanuts, replace the lemon juice with lime juice and add 1 teaspoon fish sauce (nam pla).

moroccan carrot salad
Omit the oil and mustard seeds, add 1/2 teaspoon ground cumin, 1/2 teaspoon ground cinnamon, 1 teaspoon sweet paprika, 1 crushed garlic clove and 1 green chile, finely chopped. Stir in 1 teaspoon rose harissa paste with the lemon juice before drizzling.

spicy & nutty
Add 1 finely chopped red chile with the sesame seeds and 1 tablespoon chopped pistachios.

beet, carrot & apple
Reduce the carrots to 2, add 2 peeled and grated raw beet and 2 peeled and grated apples.

variations

greek beans

see base recipe page 106

greek bean dip
Proceed with main recipe, then puree the beans in a food processor until smooth, serve with crusty bread.

smoky lima beans
Add 1 teaspoon smoked paprika to the beans at the same time as the oregano for a smoky version.

with spinach
Steam 7 cups spinach for a few minutes until wilted, stir into the beans just before serving for an additional vitamin kick.

with chorizo
Add 3/4 cup diced chorizo to the onions, and proceed with main recipe, adding 1 teaspoon smoked paprika to the mixture at the same time as the oregano.

variations

classic vinaigrette dressing

see base recipe page 107

mustard & raspberry dressing
Reduce the lemon juice by 1 lemon, omit the garlic clove and add
1 teaspoon whole-grain mustard and 1 tablespoon raspberry vinegar.
Goes well with warm chicken salad with a few fresh raspberries tossed in at
the end.

black currant & hazelnut dressing
Reduce the lemon juice by 1 lemon, omit the garlic clove and add 1
tablespoon black currant vinegar. Replace half the olive oil with hazelnut oil.

matcha ginger dressing
Add 1/4 teaspoon matcha green tea powder, 1 teaspoon miso paste, and
1 teaspoon grated fresh gingerroot to the dressing.

thai dressing
Replace the lemon juice with lime juice, replace half the olive oil with
sesame oil, omit the garlic and add 1 tablespoon fish sauce. Add 1 fresh red
chile, deseeded and finely sliced, and 1/2 teaspoon palm sugar.

variations

gado gado

see base recipe page 108

with whole-wheat soba noodles
Replace the egg noodles with whole-wheat soba noodles.

gluten-free with rice noodles
Replace the egg noodles with rice noodles.

with new potatoes
Cook 1 cup new potatoes in their skins, allow to cool, dice, toss with the vegetables and serve on the lettuce leaves.

with egg
A classic version of Gado Gado—hard boil 2 eggs, quarter and serve on the side with the lettuce leaves.

nicoise salad

see base recipe page 111

seared tuna nicoise
Replace the tinned tuna with 4 sustainably caught tuna steaks, sear them on a grill pan and serve hot on the cold salad.

chicken nicoise
Replace the tuna with 4 broiled chicken breasts, served hot or cold.

broiled salmon nicoise
Replace the tuna with 4 broiled salmon steaks, served hot or cold.

with new potatoes
Steam or boil 8 new potatoes, halve and add to the salad.

chermoula chicken salad

see base recipe page 112

white fish kebabs
Omit the chicken and cut 1 pound firm white fish into 1-inch cubes, marinating as in main recipe. Soak 4 wooden skewers in water for 20 minutes prior to use, heat the broiler to high, thread the marinated fish onto the skewers and cook, turning frequently until cooked through. Omit the sauce.

seared lamb chops
Omit the chicken and replace with 2 lamb chops per person, marinate for at least 4 hours or overnight and sear on a grill, omitting the sauce.

stuffed sardines
Omit the chicken and use the mixture to stuff and marinate sufficient sardines for 4 people, broil or grill to cook.

variations

super coleslaw

see base recipe page 114

beet coleslaw
Peel and grate a raw beet, stir into the slaw at the last minute to prevent the color seeping in and turning everything purple.

coronation coleslaw
Add 1 teaspoon madras curry powder and use lemon juice.

thai coleslaw
Omit the mustard seeds, grate in 1 inch fresh gingerroot, deseed and finely chop a red chile, add 1 tablespoon fish sauce and use lime juice.

celeriac coleslaw
Omit the apple, grate 1/2 small celeriac, 1 red onion and 1 small fennel bulb and proceed with main recipe.

main dishes

Superfoods are filling and satisfying as well as
healthy. This chapter gives you a delicious set of
dinner staples that you'll enjoy cooking and eating
over and over again.

brown rice crust quiche

see variations page 166

If you love pastry but not its high-fat, high GI composition, then this is the perfect substitute.

1 cup whole-grain basmati rice
1 medium egg
1/3 cup cheddar cheese, grated

Filling:
5 medium eggs
1/2 cup milk

1/3 cup cooked, chopped kale
1 garlic clove, finely chopped
1/3 cup cheddar cheese, grated
6 scallions, chopped
sea salt and freshly ground black pepper

Preheat the oven to 400°F (200°C). Cook the rice according to the instructions on the package. Mix the cooked rice with the egg and cheese. Grease and line a solid based 11-in. (28-cm.) round flan dish. If you only have a loose bottomed dish, make sure to line properly so that the mixture can't seep through. Press the rice mixture into the dish, pushing it up the sides of the dish to line the dish with pastry.

Bake in the oven for 25–35 minutes until golden.

Meanwhile, make the filling. Beat the eggs, mix in the milk, kale, garlic, and cheese and season well. When the base is cooked, pour in the egg and milk filling, scatter over the scallions, reduce the temperature to 350°F (180°C) and cook for a further 15–20 minutes until the egg is cooked and the filling is no longer runny.

Serves 6

kale & pistachio pesto

see variations page 167

This is the perfect quick meal on a busy evening.

3 cups kale, stem removed and chopped
1/2 cup. shelled pistachio nuts
3/4 cup parmesan, finely grated, plus extra
    to serve
2 garlic cloves, chopped

6 tbsp. extra virgin olive oil, plus extra to serve
zest and juice of 1 lemon
whole wheat, buckwheat or gluten-free
    spaghetti
chopped pistachio nuts, to serve

Place all the ingredients, except the spaghetti, in a food processor and blend to a puree. Add more extra virgin olive oil if it is too thick.

Cook the spaghetti as per the instructions on the package. To serve, stir the pesto through the spaghetti and sprinkle with a little extra parmesan, a drizzle of olive oil and a few chopped pistachio nuts.

Store the pesto covered in the refrigerator for up to 2 weeks.

Serves 8–10

sweet potato korma

see variations page 168

This mild curry is packed with goodness and much healthier as it uses coconut milk instead of cream. Serve with brown rice or whole-grain chapatti, and it's also lovely reheated for lunch the day after.

1 in. fresh gingerroot, chopped
5 garlic cloves, chopped
3 tbsp. sunflower oil
1 large onion, chopped
1 tsp. ground cumin
2 tsp. ground coriander
1 tsp. ground turmeric
5 cloves

1/2 tsp. black peppercorns
1 stick of cinnamon
4 cardamom pods
1 tsp. salt
1/2 tsp. chili powder
3 medium sweet potatoes, peeled and diced
small cauliflower, cut into florets

14-oz. can coconut milk
1/4 cup cashew nuts, blended in a food processor with a little water to make a paste
fresh cilantro, chopped
natural yogurt, to serve

Place the chopped ginger and garlic in a food processor and blend with 4 tablespoons water to make a smooth paste.

Heat the oil in a skillet. Add the chopped onion and fry for 5 minutes, until soft. Add the ginger and garlic paste, stir for 1 minute until fragrant. Add the ground cumin, coriander, turmeric, cloves, peppercorns, cinnamon, cardamom, salt, and chili powder, and cook for 2–3 minutes until fragrant. Transfer to a lidded casserole dish or saucepan, add the sweet potato, cauliflower, coconut milk, and cashew paste. Bring to a simmer, cook for 30–35 minutes until the vegetables are tender, remove from the heat and then carefully remove the cinnamon stick. To serve, sprinkle on top the chopped fresh cilantro and a dash of yogurt.

Serves 4–6

black bean chili

see variations page 169

A delicious family favorite, beans are high in protein, low in saturated fat and high in antioxidants. Black beans give a deeply rich color and flavor to this classic chili.

2 tbsp. olive oil
1 large red onion, finely diced
1 garlic clove, peeled and finely chopped
2 carrots, finely chopped
2 red bell peppers, deseeded and chopped
1 red chile, deseeded and finely chopped
1 tsp. ground cumin
1 tsp. ground coriander
14-oz. can chopped tomatoes

2 x 14-oz. cans black beans
2 tbsp. tomato paste
1/2 cup, plus 2 tbsp. vegetable broth
salt and freshly ground black pepper
1 piece of dark chocolate
small bunch fresh cilantro, chopped
avocado and lime wedges, to serve
cooked brown rice, to serve

Heat the oil in a skillet and fry the onion, garlic, carrots and peppers until starting to soften.

Transfer to a saucepan with a lid and add the chile, cumin, and coriander. Stir-fry for 1–2 minutes until you can smell the spices. Add the chopped tomatoes, drain the beans and rinse thoroughly, and add these with the tomato paste and broth. Stir, cover and bring to a simmer.

Simmer gently for 30–40 minutes until the vegetables are cooked and the sauce has thickened. Taste and add salt and pepper if necessary.

Add the chocolate and half the fresh cilantro and stir until the chocolate has melted.

Serve immediately with chunks of avocado. Scatter the remaining fresh cilantro over and place a quarter of lime and rice on the side.

Serves 4

grilled salmon with pistachio & sesame dukkah

see variations page 170

Salmon is packed full of omega 3 fatty acids, essential for cognitive function. They help to lower the risk of heart disease and arthritis. Buy wild salmon when possible.

4 wild salmon steaks
a little extra virgin olive oil
juice of 1 lemon
sea salt

Dukkah:
1/2 tsp. ground cumin
1/2 tsp. ground coriander
3 tbsp. pistachios
1 tbsp. almonds

pinch sumac
1 tbsp. sesame seeds
1/2 tsp. salt
1/2 tsp. sugar
minted pea puree, to serve

To make the dukkah, put all the ingredients in a food processor and blend, not too much as you will want the nuts to be chopped but not powdered.

Heat a grill pan until smoking hot, brush both sides of the salmon with oil, sprinkle with lemon juice and salt, and grill one side until the salmon steak has almost cooked halfway through.

Turn the salmon over, brush with a little more oil and carefully press the dukkah on the top, cooked part of the salmon. Heat the broiler, and once the salmon is almost cooked transfer the grill pan to the broiler for 1–2 minutes until the dukkah crust begins to color. Serve with minted pea puree.

Serves 4

moroccan veggie stew with harissa & couscous

see variations page 171

This lovely warming vegetable stew is bursting with goodness. It's delicious served with couscous, rice, or even a potato.

1 tsp. turmeric
pinch chili powder
2-in. stick cinnamon
pinch saffron
1 tbsp. sunflower oil
1 medium onion, peeled and cut into 8 chunks
1 in. fresh gingerroot, peeled and grated
1 sweet potato, peeled and cubed

1 medium potato, peeled and cubed
2 carrots, peeled and chopped
1 zucchini, cubed
14-oz. can chickpeas, drained and rinsed
1/4 cup raisins
salt and freshly ground black pepper
2 tbsp. fresh flat leaf parsley, washed and chopped

2 tbsp. fresh cilantro, washed and chopped, plus extra to serve
couscous, to serve
1 tsp. vegetable broth powder
1 tsp. rose harissa
juice of 2 lemons
1 tbsp. extra virgin olive oil

Mix together the turmeric, chili powder, cinnamon stick, and saffron in a small bowl.

Heat the sunflower oil in a heavy-based casserole dish or skillet. Fry the onion over a medium heat until soft. Add the ginger and stir in the dry spices, cook for 2 minutes stirring constantly until fragrant. Add the potatoes, carrot, zucchini, chickpeas, raisins and 2 cups, plus 1 tablespoon water. Bring to a boil, adding a large pinch of salt and a good pinch of black pepper. Cook, covered, for 25–30 minutes, until the vegetables are tender.

Add the parsley and cilantro and check the seasoning. Keep warm until ready to serve.

Sprinkle the couscous with 1 teaspoon of vegetable broth powder and cook according to the instructions on the package. Fluff up with a fork.

Spoon 6 tablespoons of the sauce from the stew into a small jug, add the rose harissa, lemon juice, olive oil and a good spoonful of chopped fresh cilantro and stir.

Serve the stew spooned over a mound of couscous with the harissa sauce on the side.

Serves 4

super bean burger with homemade ketchup

see variations page 172

These bean burgers are packed with flavor and are bursting with nutrients. Homemade ketchup not only tastes great but is lower in salt and sugar than store bought ketchup and is packed with antioxidants.

2 x 14-oz. cans mixed beans, drained and rinsed
1 cup breadcrumbs, whole-grain if possible
1 tbsp. Madras curry paste
1 egg, beaten
handful of fresh cilantro, chopped
sea salt and freshly ground black pepper

Spicy mayonnaise:
1 cup good quality mayonnaise
1 tsp. ground turmeric
1 tsp. ground cumin

Homemade ketchup:
3 tbsp. tomato paste
1 tbsp. dark muscovado sugar
pinch mustard powder

pinch ground cinnamon
pinch salt
pinch ground cloves
1 tbsp. white wine vinegar
a little water

whole-grain burger buns and salad, to serve

Transfer the beans to a mixing bowl and roughly mash with a potato masher or a fork, leaving some lumps for a better texture. Add the breadcrumbs, curry paste, egg, and fresh cilantro. Season with salt and pepper and stir well to mix. Wet your hands (this stops the mixture sticking) and split the mixture into 4 or 6 balls (depending how big you want the burgers to be) and flatten them gently.

Line a cookie sheet with aluminum foil, heat the broiler to high, transfer the burgers to the cookie sheet and cook under the hot broiler for 10–15 minutes, turning frequently.

To make the spicy mayonnaise, mix the mayonnaise with the turmeric and cumin and serve on the side.

To make the ketchup, whisk all the ingredients together, adding more water if it's too thick. Transfer to a clean jar and keep in the refrigerator for up to 3 days.

To serve, split and toast the burger buns, fill with a burger and top with mayo, ketchup, and salad greens. These burgers also freeze well before cooking. To heat from frozen, bake at 400°F (200°C) for 20–30 minutes.

Makes 4–6 burgers

fish fingers with sweet potato wedges & peas

see variations page 173

This is a healthy take on classic comfort food.

2 sweet potatoes
2 cups whole-grain breadcrumbs, made from
    day old stale bread or equivalent panko
    breadcrumbs
1 egg
1 lemon, zest and juice
1 tsp. dried oregano

1 tbsp. olive oil
14 oz. sustainable skinless, boneless white fish,
    sliced into 10-12 (1-in wide) strips
1 cup peas
1 tbsp. fresh mint, finely chopped
1 tbsp. crème fraiche
sea salt and freshly ground black pepper

Heat the oven to 400°F (200°C). Peel the sweet potatoes and slice into thick wedges, toss in a little oil and season with salt and pepper. Transfer to a lightly oiled baking sheet and bake for 30 minutes until golden and soft.

Spread the breadcrumbs out onto a plate, beat the egg and transfer to a shallow dish big enough to contain the fish fingers. Mix the lemon zest and oregano with the breadcrumbs and season with salt and pepper. Brush a non-stick cookie sheet with oil. Dip the fish strips into the beaten egg and then into the breadcrumbs, continue untill all the fish strips are fully coated. Transfer to the cookie sheet, then bake for 20 minutes until golden brown. Simmer the peas in a little water with the mint, mash roughly, stir in the lemon juice and crème fraiche and serve with the fish fingers and sweet potato wedges.

Serves 2-3

baked eggplant with moroccan lamb

see variations page 174

This delectable main is bursting with nutrients.

2 medium eggplants
olive oil
1 lb. ground lamb
2 tsp. paprika
1 tsp. ground cinnamon
1 tsp. ground cumin
1 tsp. ground coriander

1/2 tsp. ground fennel seeds
1/4 tsp. ground ginger
pinch ground nutmeg
pinch ground cloves
1/3 cup. pine nuts
3/4 cup cheddar cheese, grated
sea salt and freshly ground black pepper

Preheat the oven to 400°F (200°C). Slice the eggplant lengthways and lay, cut-side-up, on a cookie sheet. Brush with olive oil and season. Bake for 20–25 minutes until soft and golden.

Meanwhile, cook the lamb, sprinkle over the spices, season and fry in a skillet until browned. Stir in the pine nuts.

Remove the eggplant from the oven, pile over the lamb, sprinkle with cheese, and return to the oven for 5 minutes until the cheese has melted before serving.

Serves 4

lemon chicken with quinoa & spinach

see variations page 175

High in protein, this is a perfect light meal.

2 unwaxed lemons
8 chicken thighs, on the bone with skin on
olive oil
2 garlic cloves, lightly crushed in their skins
small bunch fresh lemon thyme

3 cups chicken broth
1 cup quinoa
2 cups spinach
sea salt and freshly ground black pepper

Preheat the oven to gas 400°F (200°C). Halve one of the lemons lengthways and slice it so you have "half moon" shapes. Lay the chicken thighs, skin side up in a roasting pan, cut a slash into the tops and insert a slice of lemon. Drizzle with olive oil, sprinkle with sea salt and freshly ground black pepper, tuck the crushed garlic cloves under some of the chicken at either end of the roasting pan and scatter over the fresh thyme. Roast for 30-40 minutes until cooked through.

Meanwhile, heat the chicken broth, rinse the quinoa in plenty of fresh water and tip into the broth. Bring to a simmer, cover and cook for 15–20 minutes until the quinoa has absorbed most of the broth. Add the spinach and finely grated zest of the remaining lemon and continue cooking for 5 minutes until the spinach has wilted and the quinoa is tender. Squeeze over the juice from the remaining lemon, season and stir to mix. Serve with the roast chicken thighs.

Serves 4

chicken breasts with harissa, spinach & mozzarella

see variations page 176

These are equally good as a family supper or to cook for friends as an informal supper party.

4 cups spinach
4 chicken breasts, bone in, skin on
2–3 tsp. rose harissa
1 ball buffalo mozzarella, sliced

20 cherry tomatoes on the vine
olive oil
sea salt and freshly ground black pepper
salad or couscous, to serve

Steam the spinach for 3–4 minutes until just wilted, remove from the heat.

Preheat the oven to 375°F (190°C), lay the chicken breasts on an oiled cookie sheet and loosen the skin.

Lift the skin and spread the rose harissa on the chicken breasts between the flesh and the skin. Spread the spinach on top and lay the mozzarella on top of the spinach, season well. Replace the skin, stretching it over the chicken and topping, lay the cherry tomatoes next to the chicken and drizzle everything with olive oil and season.

Roast for 20–25 minutes until the chicken is cooked through and serve with salad or couscous.

Serves 4

roasted butternut squash with red onion, feta & pomegranate

see variations page 177

This meal works well as a lunch or dinner and is high in beta carotene, a nutrient known for its beneficial skin-healing properties.

1 butternut squash, sliced into wedges
2 red onions, peeled and thickly sliced
olive oil
3/4 cup feta cheese
1/2 cup pomegranate seeds

1 tbsp. ground sumac
extra virgin olive oil, for drizzling
sea salt and freshly ground black pepper
seeded, kamut or millet bread, to serve

Preheat the oven to 400°F (200°C). Place the butternut squash wedges and red onion slices on a cookie sheet, brush with olive oil and season. Bake for 20–25 minutes until tender and just browning at the edges.

Put the squash and onion on a plate, crumble over the feta cheese and sprinkle with pomegranate seeds and sumac. Drizzle with extra virgin olive oil and serve with seeded, kamut or millet bread.

Serves 2

fish cakes

see variations page 178

These are so easy to make, and a great way to get more fish into your diet.

2 large potatoes	4 eggs, beaten
2 small skinless salmon fillets	2 cups whole-grain flour
4 cups almond or dairy milk	2 cups whole-grain breadcrumbs
1 bay leaf	olive oil, to brush
2 tbsp. butter	sea salt and freshly ground black pepper

Preheat the oven to 350°F (180°C). Peel and chop the potatoes then boil them in a saucepan for 15–20 minutes until tender. Meanwhile, place the salmon fillets in an oven proof dish, cover with the milk, add the bay leaf, season and bake for 10–15 minutes until the fish is cooked through. Remove from the oven and flake the fish, removing all bones. Reserve the milk.

Drain the potatoes and mash with the butter and a little of the warm milk in which the fish was cooked. Add the fish and sufficient egg to bind the mixture together. Form the mixture into balls and flatten them to make small patties.

Raise the oven temperature to 400°F (200°C). Put the flour in a shallow bowl, the remaining egg in another small bowl and the breadcrumbs on a plate. Coat each fish cake in flour, dunk in the egg and finally in the breadcrumbs. Lay the fish cakes on a cookie sheet, brush with a little oil and bake for 10–15 minutes, turning over halfway. Serve with green vegetables and homemade ketchup (see page 138).

Serves 2–3

barley risotto with beet

see variations page 179

This dish is as pretty as it is delicious.

3 medium beets
4 cups chicken or vegetable broth
1 1/2 tbsp. butter
2 tbsp. olive oil
1 large onion, finely chopped
2 garlic cloves, finely chopped

1 3/4 cups pearl barley
1 tbsp. fresh thyme
zest and juice of 1 lemon
1 cup hard goat cheese
sea salt and freshly ground black pepper

Peel and grate the beet, use gloves if you don't want to get pink fingers. Bring the broth to a simmer. Heat the butter and oil in a large saucepan, add the onion and cook over a medium heat for 3–4 minutes until softening, add the garlic and cook for another minute.

Add the barley and stir to coat. Add the grated beet, thyme, and half the broth, simmer until the broth has been absorbed. Add the remaining broth a ladle at a time making sure that it has been absorbed before adding more. Keep checking that the barley is tender, it will take longer than rice so expect 30–40 minutes and stop adding broth when it is tender.

Season with salt and pepper, stir in the lemon zest and juice, crumble in the goat cheese, and sprinkle over to serve.

Serves 4

whole-wheat pasta bake

see variations page 180

Heavenly comfort food that's good for you.

3 cups whole-wheat or spelt
    penne pasta
olive oil
1 red onion, finely diced
1 carrot, grated
1 red bell pepper, finely diced
1 zucchini, grated

14-oz. can chopped tomatoes
4 tbsp. crème fraiche
1/3 cup parmesan, grated plus
    extra to serve
1/2 cup mozzarella, cubed,
    plus 1 ball, sliced

1 cup cherry tomatoes, halved
bunch fresh basil leaves
sea salt and freshly ground
    black pepper

Preheat the oven to 400°F (200°C). Cook the pasta in plenty of boiling salted water until al dente. Meanwhile, heat a little olive oil in a skillet and sauté the red onion for 4–5 minutes until starting to soften. Add the grated carrot, bell pepper, and zucchini and cook for a further 5 minutes. Stir in the tomatoes and leave to simmer for 10 minutes until all the vegetables are soft. Blend to a puree using an immersion blender. Return to the saucepan and add the crème fraiche and grated parmesan. Stir to mix.

Drain the pasta and add to the tomato sauce. Fold in the mozzarella cubes and cherry tomatoes, add a tablespoon of chopped fresh basil, season and place in an oiled baking dish. Spread over the sliced mozzarella discs. Bake for 20–25 minutes until the cheese is bubbly. Chop the rest of the basil, sprinkle over and serve.

Serves 4–6

lamb meatballs with tahini sauce

see variations page 181

These are lovely served with salads, coleslaw, or tabbouleh or stuffed into pita with crispy lettuce and chopped tomatoes.

1 lb. lean ground lamb
1 tbsp. fresh oregano, chopped
2 tsp. pomegranate molasses
sea salt and freshly ground black pepper

Sauce:
2 tbsp. tahini paste
juice of 2 lemons
water

Mix together the ground lamb, chopped oregano, 1 teaspoon pomegranate molasses and a good pinch of salt and pepper. Squeeze the ground meat together and roll into 16–20 walnut-sized balls.

Place in a skillet (you won't need any oil as the lamb will produce a lot on its own) and cook, turning frequently until cooked through and lightly browned on the outside. If the lamb produces a lot of oil then tip some of it out of the skillet.

Combine the ingredients for the tahini sauce, adding lemon juice to taste and sufficient water to create a thick pouring consistency.

Serve the meatballs with the remaining pomegranate molasses and a drizzle of tahini sauce.

Serves 4

oven baked mackerel with wilted greens

see variations page 182

Rich in omega 3 and 6 fatty acids, this dish is truly super!

4 whole mackerel, descaled, gutted, and cleaned
olive oil
2 lemons
3 cups kale, stem removed and finely sliced

3 cups spinach, finely sliced
bunch of tarragon
sea salt and freshly ground black pepper

Preheat the oven to 375°F (190°C). Line a cookie sheet with aluminum foil and oil lightly. Pat the mackerel dry and lay on the cookie sheet. Slice one of the lemons into 4 thick slices.

Brush the mackerel with oil, sprinkle with sea salt and freshly ground black pepper. Place a thick slice of lemon and a sprig of tarragon inside each mackerel. Cover with aluminum foil and roast for 15–20 minutes until cooked.

Meanwhile, steam the kale and spinach until wilted, remove from the heat, sprinkle with sea salt, pepper, and squeeze over juice from the remaining lemon. Serve immediately.

Serves 4

superfood lasagna

see variations page 183

Lasagna is a family staple and perfect comfort food for autumnal evenings. Enjoy this version knowing that it's actually good for you.

Bolognese sauce:
1 tbsp. olive oil
1 red onion, finely chopped
1 garlic clove, finely chopped
1 lb. lean ground beef
1 red bell pepper, chopped
1 cup mushrooms, chopped
14-oz. can chopped tomatoes
1 tbsp. tomato paste
1/2 cup, plus 2 tbsp. water
2 tsp. Worcestershire sauce

1 1/2 cups spinach
1 tbsp. fresh basil, roughly torn

Cheese sauce:
1 1/2 tablespoons butter
3 tbsp. spelt flour
1 cup 2 percent or soy milk
2 cups mature cheddar cheese, grated

whole-grain spelt lasagna sheets
sea salt and freshly ground black pepper
grated parmesan cheese, to serve
green salad, to serve

Heat the oil in a skillet and sauté the onions and garlic over a gentle heat for 5–10 minutes until translucent. Add the ground beef, season and cook until browned. Transfer to a lidded saucepan and set over a low heat. Add the red bell pepper and mushrooms to the skillet and sauté for a few minutes until beginning to soften, add to the beef.

Pour in the chopped tomatoes, tomato paste, water, and Worcestershire sauce, mix well and bring to a boil. Cover, reduce to a simmer, and cook for 30–45 minutes until the meat is cooked through.

To make the cheese sauce, melt the butter in a saucepan, add the flour and stir over a low heat with a wooden spoon for 2-3 minutes to make sure the flour is cooked. Gradually add

the milk, stirring until it has been incorporated before adding more. Continue to add the milk a little at a time until it has all been incorporated and you have a smooth and glossy sauce. If you have lumps, whisk well. Remove from the heat and stir in the grated cheese.

Cook the lasagna sheets per the instructions on the package. Remove the meat from the heat, add the spinach and basil, and stir well to wilt.

Assemble the lasagna by layering a little of the meat sauce in the bottom of a heat proof dish, cover with lasagna sheets, and continue until you have 3 layers of meat and lasagna. Pour the cheese sauce over the final, third lasagna layer. Sprinkle with grated parmesan cheese and cook in the oven for 20–30 minutes until piping hot and the cheese topping is nicely browned. Serve with a green salad.

Serves 4

shepherd's pie with sweet potato mash

see variations page 184

This British classic is a wholesome meal, low in fat and high in nutrients.

2 sweet potatoes
olive oil
1 onion, finely chopped
1 lb. ground lamb
14-oz. can chopped tomatoes
1 tbsp. tomato paste

1 cup beef or vegetable broth
1/2 cup peas, fresh or frozen
2 carrots, grated
1 tsp. dried oregano
sea salt and freshly ground black pepper

Preheat the oven to 430°F (220°C). Prick the sweet potatoes with a fork and bake for 35–40 minutes until soft.

Heat the oil in a skillet, add the onion and cook over a low heat until softened. Add the lamb, season and cook until browned. Transfer the lamb to a lidded saucepan or casserole dish, stir in the tomatoes, paste, broth, peas, carrots and oregano. Mix well and bring to a boil. Season, cover and simmer for 30 minutes.

Meanwhile, scoop out the sweet potatoes from their skins, mash, and turn the oven down to 350°F (180°C). Once the lamb is cooked, transfer to an oven proof dish, spread over the sweet potatoes and bake for 20 minutes until the potato is golden brown and the dish is piping hot. Serve with steamed green vegetables.

Serves 4

kashmiri chicken & spinach curry

see variations page 185

Packed with flavor, this curry is also delicious reheated for lunch the next day.

4 chicken breasts, skinless
    and boneless
1 tsp. coriander seeds
1 tsp. cumin seeds
1 tbsp. sunflower oil
1 large onion, finely chopped
2 in. fresh gingerroot,
    chopped

3 garlic cloves, chopped
1 green chile, deseeded and
    chopped
5 cardamom pods
1 tsp. turmeric
1 bay leaf
bunch fresh cilantro, chopped
3/4 cup slivered almonds

1 cup organic yogurt
1 1/2 cups spinach
sea salt and freshly ground
    black pepper
cooked brown rice, to serve

Cut the chicken breasts into chunks. Heat a heavy saucepan until smoking hot, tip in the coriander and cumin seeds and dry fry for 1–2 minutes until toasted and fragrant. Transfer to a pestle and mortar and grind to a powder.

Heat the oil in the saucepan, add the onion and cook until softened. Put the ginger and garlic cloves in a food processor with 4–5 tablespoons water and blend to a paste. Add to the onion and cook for 2 minutes until fragrant. Add the freshly ground coriander and cumin seeds with the green chile, cardamom, turmeric, and bay leaf and cook for 2–3 minutes until fragrant. Add half the fresh cilantro. Add the chicken and stir well to coat. Add the almonds, yogurt and seasoning. Bring to a simmer, cover and cook for 45 minutes until the chicken is cooked through. Stir in the spinach and remaining fresh cilantro. Serve with brown rice.

Serves 4

sweet potato gnocchi with roast cherry tomato sauce

see variations page 186

This can be a little time-consuming to prepare but the results are well worth the effort.

1 small sweet potato
2 white potatoes
1 1/2 cups all-purpose flour
1 egg
sea salt and freshly ground
    black pepper
arugula leaves, to serve

Sauce:
2 cups cherry tomatoes
2 red onions, finely chopped
1 garlic clove, finely chopped
1 tbsp. olive oil
1/2 cup fresh basil

sea salt and freshly ground
    black pepper
freshly grated parmesan to
    serve

Bake the sweet potatoes and white potatoes in their skins until soft. Alternatively you could peel and cube the potatoes and steam them, do not boil the potatoes as they will soak up too much water and you will have soggy gnocchi that is difficult to mix. Scoop out the potato flesh and mash together until very smooth.

Add the flour, egg and salt and pepper and mix to form a firm dough. Knead the dough for 1–2 minutes then roll out into a sausage 1/2-in thick. Cut into 1-in pieces, gently rolling each piece down the back of a fork to make indentations on the gnocchi. Transfer to a floured cookie sheet and continue with the rest of the dough. Cover and chill until ready to use.

To make the sauce, preheat the oven to 430°F (220°C), put the tomatoes, chopped onions

and garlic on a cookie sheet and drizzle over the olive oil. Mix together with your hands to make sure all the vegetables are covered. Tear the basil leaves into 3–4 pieces and toss over the tomatoes, season and bake for 20 minutes, or until the tomatoes have burst.

To cook the gnocchi, bring a large saucepan of salted water to the boil, add a few gnocchi at a time (they take around 2 minutes to cook and will rise to the top of the saucepan when they are cooked). Continue until all the gnocchi are cooked.

Serve on a bed of arugula with the cherry tomato sauce and a good sprinkling of parmesan cheese and black pepper, if desired.

Serves 4

superfood fajitas

see variations page 187

A superfood take on classic fajitas, use good quality steak and cook it to your liking.
Steak is high in iron which is great for boosting your immune system.

1 tbsp. olive oil
1 lb. rump or sirloin steak
2 red onions, finely sliced
3 bell peppers, various colors,
    finely sliced
1 1/2 cups mushrooms, finely
    sliced
1 tsp. chili powder

3 limes
2 cups baby or purple
    sprouting broccoli
small bunch of fresh cilantro,
    finely chopped
3 ripe tomatoes, a mixture of
    red, yellow and purple
sea salt and freshly ground

black pepper
4 whole-grain tortilla wraps
guacamole, sour cream, grated
    cheese, to serve

Heat some of the oil in a skillet, add the steak and cook to your own taste. Set aside to rest.
Heat a little more oil and add the sliced onions, bell peppers, and mushrooms, sprinkle in the
chili powder and juice of 1 lime and fry until just "catching" at the edges. At the same time
steam the broccoli until just tender and drain.

Slice the steak, add this to the skillet with the vegetables, stir to coat. Add the broccoli and
gently stir. Stir in the chopped fresh cilantro.

Plunge the tomatoes into boiling water for 1 minute, drain and remove the skins. Halve,
remove the seeds and dice, sprinkle with the juice of a lime and a little salt. Warm the
tortillas and serve with guacamole, sour cream, grated cheese and the tomato salsa.

Serves 4

dhal

see variations page 188

Dhal is a lentil based dish, high in protein so it's very good for you and counts as one of your portions of fruit and veg. Dhal makes a great base for a nutrient packed lunch that can be reheated at work with the addition of other leftovers.

1 cup red lentils
1 in. fresh gingerroot
1 cinnamon stick
1 1/2 tbsp. butter
1 onion, finely sliced

2 garlic cloves, finely sliced
1 tsp. ground turmeric
1 tsp. ground cumin
1/2 tsp. ground garam masala
1/2 tsp. chili flakes (optional)

juice of 2 lemons
1/2 tsp. salt
1 tbsp. fresh cilantro, chopped

Place the lentils in a saucepan with 2 1/2 cups water and bring to a boil. Grate the fresh gingerroot and add to the saucepan along with the cinnamon stick. Simmer for 10 minutes, making sure you keep an eye on it to ensure it doesn't "catch" on the bottom of the saucepan, if it does add a little more water.

Melt the butter in a skillet and add the finely sliced onion, cook for 3–4 minutes then add the garlic, turmeric, cumin, garam masala, and chile flakes if using. If you like spicy food then you can double the amount of chili if you wish. Cook for 3–4 minutes until the onion is caramelized then add to the dhal.

Stir together and add the lemon juice and salt and cook for a further 3 minutes. Stir in the fresh cilantro and serve.

Serves 4–6

quesadillas with whole-grain tortillas

see variations page 189

Mexican-style toasted sandwiches that can be filled with tasty nutritious morsels.

1 red onion, finely chopped
2 garlic cloves, finely chopped
Coconut or sunflower oil
1 tsp. cumin seeds
14-oz. can pinto beans
2 tsp. smoked paprika
juice of 2 limes

4 whole-grain tortilla wraps
1 cup strong cheddar, grated
small bunch cilantro, chopped
sour cream
handful of cherry tomatoes, chopped
jalapeño chiles, deseeded and sliced
sea salt and freshly ground black pepper

Gently fry the onion and garlic in oil for 2-3 minutes, add the cumin seeds and cook for another minute. Drain and rinse the beans and tip these into the pan with the paprika and a tablespoon of water. Mash the beans roughly with a potato masher or a fork to make a chunky puree, season with salt and pepper, add a good squeeze of lime juice, and mix well.

Lay the tortillas flat, spread a quarter of the bean mixture on half the tortilla, sprinkle with grated cheese, a little chopped cilantro, sour cream, a few cherry tomatoes and some sliced chiles. Sprinkle over more lime juice then fold over the half of the tortilla without any filling and fold the whole thing over again into quarters. Repeat with the other tortillas.

Heat a little oil in a grill or skillet and cook each quesadilla for 1-2 minutes until they are crisp and the cheese melts. Turn over and cook the other side, serve warm with sour cream.

Serves 4

cauliflower base pizza

see variations page 190

Fabulous for low-carb or gluten-free diets.

1 medium raw cauliflower
1 medium egg
1/4 cup parmesan, grated
1 tsp. dried oregano
2 balls mozzarella cheese

olive oil
1 1/2 tbsp. pureed tomato
salt and freshly ground black pepper
selection of toppings

Preheat the oven to 400°F (200°C). Grate the cauliflower, discarding the stalk and hard center. Place in a microwave safe container and cook in the microwave on high for 4 minutes. Tip the grated cauliflower into a clean towel or piece of muslin and let cool. Once cool, squeeze out the water from the grated cauliflower.

Tip the cauliflower into a bowl, add the egg, grated parmesan and oregano. Grate half a ball of mozzarella, season well, add to the cauliflower and mix. Split the mixture into two and gently squeeze each half into a ball to make two pizza bases.

Sprinkle a little olive oil onto a piece of parchment or cookie sheet and flatten each ball into a round on the oiled tray or parchment. Neaten the edges and bake for 10 minutes until golden brown. Remove from the oven and spread over the pureed tomato and other toppings of your choice, scatter with the remaining mozzarella and bake for 6–10 minutes until the cheese is bubbling.

Serves 2

roasted veg tarts with spelt cheat's puff pastry

see variations page 191

Fabulous for low-carb or gluten-free diets.

2 cups spelt flour
1 cup unsalted butter, cubed
1/2 cup sour cream
pinch salt
1 eggplant
1 zucchini

1 red bell pepper
1 orange bell pepper
1 red onion
20 cherry tomatoes
olive oil
fresh thyme and rosemary

1 egg, beaten
1/3 cup feta or goat cheese
sea salt and freshly ground
   black pepper

Put the flour and cubed butter in a food processor and process until it resembles breadcrumbs. Add the sour cream and salt and process once again until the mixture forms a ball. Transfer to a freezer bag and chill for an hour before use.

Preheat the oven to 400°F (200°C). Dice the vegetables, lay on a greased cookie sheet, drizzle with olive oil, scatter over the herbs and season. Roast for 20–25 minutes until soft and just starting to catch at the edges.

On a sheet of lightly floured baking parchment, roll out the pastry into an oblong shape. Score around the edge and bake for 10–15 minutes until just golden. Remove from the oven, brush with the egg to seal the pastry and bake for another 5 minutes. Top with the roasted vegetables, season and sprinkle over the feta or goat cheese. Bake for 5–10 minutes until golden brown and warmed through and serve.

Serves 4–6

variations

brown rice crust quiche

see base recipe page 127

with spinach & feta
Replace the kale with the same quantity of cooked spinach and the cheddar cheese in the filling with the same quantity of crumbled feta cheese.

with broccoli, peas & zucchini
Replace the kale with 1/3 cup steamed broccoli tips, 1 tablespoon cooked peas and 10 thin slices of zucchini.

roasted tomato, red onion & parmesan
Omit the kale, roast 1/2 cup cherry tomatoes and 1 small red onion, peeled and cut into eighths, in a little oil for 20 minutes until just beginning to char. Stir into the egg mixture and replace the cheddar with the same quantity of grated parmesan.

with watercress & goat cheese
Replace the kale with the same quantity of watercress and the cheddar with the same quantity of crumbled goat cheese.

kale & pistachio pesto

see base recipe page 128

classic pesto
Replace the kale and pistachio nuts with a large bunch of basil and 1/3 cup toasted pine nuts.

sun-dried tomato pesto
Make classic pesto above and add 8 drained and chopped sun-dried tomatoes.

beet & walnut pesto
Replace the kale with 1 cooked beet, the pistachio nuts with 3/4 cup walnuts (toasted in a dry skillet) and reduce the parmesan to1/2 cup.

purple sprouting broccoli pesto
Replace the kale with 1 3/4 cups purple sprouting broccoli, add a small bunch of basil and replace the pistachio nuts with toasted pine nuts.

variations

sweet potato korma

see base recipe page 131

root vegetable korma
Reduce the sweet potatoes by 1 or 2 and add 2 medium carrots and
2 medium parsnips.

chicken & chickpea korma
You could leave out the chickpeas but that would reduce the "superfood"
quality. Omit the sweet potatoes and cauliflower, dice 4 chicken breasts
and add to the fragrant spices, cooking until just colored before adding the
coconut milk.

mixed vegetable korma
Replace the sweet potatoes and cauliflower with 1 eggplant, diced, 1 small
butternut squash, peeled and diced, 1/2 cup green beans, and 1/2 cup okra.
Add the green beans and okra 5 minutes before the end of the cooking time.

almond korma
Replace the cashew nuts with the same quantity of almonds.

variations

black bean chili

see base recipe page 132

three bean chili
Replace one of the cans of black beans with kidney beans and add a can of black eyed peas. Serves 6.

chili con carne & chipotle
Replace 1 can black beans with 2 cups lean ground beef or diced steak, brown the meat before adding the tomatoes and beans. Add 1 dried, crumbled chipotle chile in place of the chili powder or stir in 1 teaspoon chipotle paste before serving.

sweet potato chili
Replace 1 can black beans with 1 diced sweet potato.

with quinoa
Stir in 1/3 cup quinoa 20 minutes before the end of the cooking time, serve with whole-grain flatbread or whole-grain pita.

variations

grilled salmon with pistachio & sesame dukkah

see base recipe page 135

harissa salmon with hazelnut dukkah
Replace the pistachios and almonds with 4 tablespoons hazelnuts and smear the top of each salmon steak with rose harissa, top with the dukkah.

olive & sun-dried tomato salmon with almond dukkah
Replace the pistachios with an additional 3 tablespoons of almonds, smear the top of each salmon steak with olive and sun-dried tomato tapenade, top with the dukkah.

salmon with sweet paprika dukkah
Add 1 teaspoon fennel seeds and 1 teaspoon sweet paprika to the dukkah mix.

salmon with fragrant seedy dukkah
Add 1 tablespoon pumpkin seeds, 1 tablespoon sunflower seeds, 1/2 tablespoon poppy seeds, 2 teaspoons dried thyme, and a large pinch of oregano to to the dukkah, reducing the pistachios to 1 tablespoon.

moroccan veggie stew with harissa & couscous

see base recipe page 136

with lentils & apricots
Add 1/3 cup lentils to the dish when adding the chickpeas and replace the raisins with 5 chopped dried apricots. You may need to add a little extra water but check 15 minutes after adding the lentils.

sweet potato & butternut squash
Omit the potato, carrots and zucchini and replace with an additional sweet potato and 1 small butternut squash, diced.

butternut squash, bell peppers & apricots
Omit the potato, carrot and zucchini and replace with 1 small butternut squash, 1 yellow bell pepper, 1 orange bell pepper and 1 red bell pepper, all diced, and replace the raisins with 5 chopped dried apricots.

tomatoes & dates
Reduce the broth to 1 cup and add a 14-oz can of chopped tomatoes, replacing the raisins with 4 pitted chopped dates.

variations

super bean burger with homemade ketchup

see base recipe page 138

english bean burgers
Replace the curry paste with tomato paste, top with slices of red onion, a smear of English mustard and homemade ketchup.

mexican burgers
Replace the curry paste with 2 teaspoons chipotle paste, serve with a slaw made with lime juice and top with a slice of avocado and some tomato salsa.

italian burgers
Replace the curry paste with a finely chopped red bell pepper or 2 chopped bell peppers from a jar. Replace the fresh cilantro with fresh basil and serve with a slice of mozzarella and smear of fresh pesto.

fish fingers with sweet potato wedges & peas

see base recipe page 140

with salmon
Replace the white fish with the same quantity of salmon.

with root vegetable mash
Steam 1 sweet potato, 1 carrot and 1 small potato until tender, mash with a little butter, season and serve with the fish fingers.

with beet french fries
Omit the sweet potatoes and replace with 2-3 peeled beets cut into wedges, cook as before.

with classic french fries
Replace the sweet potatoes with standard potatoes and cook as before.

baked eggplant with moroccan lamb

see base recipe page 141

with roasted bell peppers
Roast 2 quartered red bell peppers with the eggplant, chop finely, and stir into the ground lamb.

with spicy chickpeas & tahini
Omit the lamb, drain and rinse 2 x 14-oz cans of chickpeas, sprinkle over the spices, and warm these through. Scoop out some of the flesh of the eggplant, chop and add to the chickpeas and pine nuts then pile the mixture back into the eggplant halves and proceed with main recipe. Drizzle with tahini sauce (see page 150).

with roasted mixed veg
Omit the lamb, with the eggplant roast 4 bell peppers, quartered (different colors if possible) 1/2 cup cherry tomatoes, 1 red onion cut into eighths. Chop and add to a saucepan with the spices and pine nuts, heat through, pile onto the eggplant halves and proceed with main recipe.

lemon chicken with quinoa & spinach

see base recipe page 142

with sun-dried tomatoes & kale
Replace the spinach with 2 cups kale, chopped and stalks removed. Proceed with main recipe, adding 8 drained, chopped sun-dried tomatoes to the quinoa at the same time as the kale.

with feta cheese & black olives
Proceed with main recipe, adding 1/4 cup black olives to the quinoa at the same time as the spinach and crumbling 1/4 cup feta cheese over the quinoa to serve.

with couscous
Replace the quinoa with the same quantity of couscous, stir the spinach into the couscous and pour over sufficient hot chicken broth to cover the couscous allowing around 1-in of broth over the top of the couscous. Cover with a clean towel and leave for 5–10 minutes until the couscous has soaked up all the broth. Fluff with a fork and serve.

chicken breasts with harissa, spinach & mozzarella

see base recipe page 144

italian version with pesto
Replace the rose harissa and spinach with pesto. Serve with a few toasted pine nuts scattered on top with some buckwheat pasta and salad.

tapenade & goat cheese
Replace the rose harissa with tapenade and the mozzarella with a slice of goat cheese.

sun-dried tomatoes & cream cheese
Replace the rose harissa with 8 chopped sun-dried tomatoes and spread over cream cheese in place of the mozzarella. Omit the spinach and replace with a few fresh basil leaves.

roasted butternut squash with red onion, feta, & pomegranate

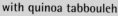

see base recipe page 145

with quinoa tabbouleh

Make Quinoa Tabbouleh (see page 97) serve with the butternut squash piled on the tabbouleh and reduce the feta cheese to 1/2 cup.

with sweet potato

Replace the butternut squash with 2 medium sweet potatoes. Bake whole, halve, and pile the feta cheese and pomegranate on top.

with roasted beets

Peel 2–3 small beets and cut into quarters, roast with the butternut squash and serve piled with the butternut squash wedges. Serves 3–4.

variations

fish cakes

see base recipe page 147

with mackerel & spinach
Replace the salmon with two skinless smoked mackerel fillets. Steam
1 cup spinach for a few minutes until wilted and stir into the
mashed potato.

gluten-free
Omit the breadcrumbs, replace the flour with gluten-free flour and form the
patties, omitting the breadcrumb stage. Brush with oil and bake.

with cod & sweet potato
Replace the salmon with one medium cod fillet. Replace half the potato
with sweet potato and proceed with main recipe.

with canned tuna or salmon
Replace the salmon fillet with 2 x 5-oz. cans tuna or salmon in water, drain
and add to the mashed potato before proceeding with main recipe.

barley risotto with beet

see base recipe page 148

with asparagus
Steam 1/2 cup asparagus spears and gently stir into the risotto just before serving.

with spinach
Omit the beet and proceed with main recipe. Steam 1 1/2 cups spinach, blend in a food processor and add to the risotto when all the liquid has been absorbed and it's almost ready to serve, warm through for 2–3 minutes and serve.

variations

whole-wheat pasta bake

see base recipe page 149

with artichokes
Add 1 jar of drained, rinsed artichoke hearts at the same time as the cream. Proceed with main recipe.

with chicken & spinach
Add 1 cup cooked, diced chicken at the same time as the mozzarella and 1 cup cooked spinach at the same time as the cherry tomatoes. Proceed with main recipe.

with salmon
Add 2 cans of salmon or 2 cooked salmon steaks, flaked, to the pasta at the same time as the cherry tomatoes. Proceed with main recipe.

with tuna
Add 2 cans of sustainably caught tuna in spring water or 2 cooked sustainably caught tuna steaks, flaked, to the pasta at the same time as the cherry tomatoes. Proceed with main recipe.

variations

lamb meatballs with tahini sauce

see base recipe page 150

spicy version
Add 1 teaspoon sweet paprika and either 1 hot fresh red chile, finely diced,
or 1 teaspoon hot chili powder. Serve with a cool yogurt dressing made of
2–3 tablespoons yogurt mixed with a little freshly squeezed lemon juice and
a sprinkle of sweet paprika.

cumin & coriander meatballs
Omit the oregano and pomegranate molasses, replace with 1 teaspoon each
coriander seeds and cumin seeds, dry fried and roughly ground in a pestle
and mortar.

harissa meatballs
Replace the oregano with mint and add 1 teaspoon each coriander seeds
and cumin seeds, dry fried and roughly ground in a pestle and mortar, plus
2 teaspoons rose harissa paste and serve with couscous.

greek meatballs
Replace the oregano with mint, omit the pomegranate molasses and serve
with tzatziki made by peeling, grating and draining the flesh of a cucumber
and stirring in 3 tablespoons Greek yogurt, 1/2 tablespoon fresh chopped
mint and a little lemon juice.

oven baked mackerel with wilted greens

see base recipe page 153

baked stuffed mackerel
Replace the sliced lemon and tarragon with a bunch of fresh mixed herbs such as oregano, bay, parsley, and thyme. Place a bunch into each mackerel and proceed with main recipe.

with roasted veg couscous
Dice 1 zucchini, 1 red onion, and 1 red bell pepper, drizzle with oil, and roast on a separate cookie sheet to the mackerel. Stir into cooked couscous along with a squeeze of lemon juice and serve with the mackerel.

day after mackerel pâté
If you have mackerel left over, remove the bones and mash the flesh with a little Greek yogurt and lemon juice for a delicious pâté.

variations

superfood lasagna

see base recipe page 154

gluten-free
Replace the spelt lasagna with gluten-free lasagna and the flour with gluten-free flour and proceed with main recipe.

roast vegetable
Omit the ground beef and replace with 1 eggplant, 1 zucchini, 1 orange bell pepper and 1 1/2 cups butternut squash, diced and roasted in 1 tablespoon olive oil in a hot oven for 20 minutes. Add to the chopped tomatoes and proceed with main recipe.

turkey & mushroom
Omit the sauce, make an additional quantity of cheese sauce. Sauté 1 pound diced turkey with the onion, sauté 1 cup sliced portobello mushrooms, stir into the cheese sauce and layer with the lasagna.

variations

shepherd's pie with sweet potato mash

see base recipe page 156

with sweet potato, potato & leek
If you prefer a less sweet version of the topping, reduce the sweet potatoes by half, replace with 2 baked potatoes, mashed. Sauté 1 diced leek in a little butter and add to the mash before spreading over the ground lamb, top with 1/4 cup grated cheese and finish in the oven.

with butternut squash mash
Replace the sweet potato with the same quantity of roasted or steamed butternut squash, mashed.

with rosti topping
Replace the sweet potato with the same quantity of grated potato, fried in a mixture of olive oil and butter until almost crispy, top the ground lamb with the rosti topping and finish in the oven.

with purple mash
Replace the sweet potato with 2 cups cooked potato and 1 1/2 cups cooked beet. Mash the potato and beet together with a little milk if required and top the ground lamb.

cottage pie
Replace the ground lamb with the same quantity of ground beef.

variations

kashmiri chicken & spinach curry

see base recipe page 157

with eggplant & peanuts
Omit the spinach and almonds, dice 1 eggplant, brown the pieces with the onion before adding the ginger-garlic paste. Chop 3/4 cup roasted peanuts in a food processor and add to the curry in place of the almonds.

with lamb
Omit the chicken and replace with 4 lean lamb leg steaks, diced. Brown the diced lamb before frying the onion, remove from the skillet and add again at the same time as the fresh cilantro.

vegetable
Omit the chicken and replace with 1 diced eggplant, 2 diced zucchini and a 14-oz can of drained, rinsed chickpeas.

variations

sweet potato gnocchi with roast cherry tomato sauce

see base recipe page 158

spinach gnocchi
Replace the sweet potato with the same quantity of potato. Chop 3 cups fresh spinach and add to the potato at the same time as the flour. Proceed with main recipe.

beet gnocchi
Omit the sweet potato and increase the white potatoes to 3. Puree 1/2 cooked beet in a food processor and add to the mashed potato. Proceed with main recipe.

gluten-free gnocchi
Replace the flour in any of the recipes with 1 1/4 cups rice flour.

gorgonzola sauce
Replace the cherry tomato sauce with 1/2 cup gorgonzola cheese melted in a saucepan over a low heat with 1/4 cup heavy cream. Serve with any of the gnocchi recipes on a bed of arugula with the sauce drizzled over, finished with freshly grated parmesan cheese.

variations

superfood fajitas

see base recipe page 161

chicken fajitas
Replace the steak with 4 chicken breasts.

lamb fajitas
Replace the steak with 4 lamb leg steaks.

vegetable fajitas
Omit the steak and add 14-oz can drained and rinsed black or borlotti beans.

variations

dhal

see base recipe page 162

spicy cauliflower veg pot
Parboil the florets from a head of cauliflower for 3–4 minutes, drain well and leave to dry totally. Preheat the oven to 400°F (200°C), crush two garlic cloves in 2 tablespoons olive oil and mix well. Brush the cauliflower florets with the garlic oil, put on the cookie sheet and roast for 8–10 minutes until just starting to brown. Stir into the dhal, adding a little more water to thin it down and serve.

with chicken
Stir in leftover roast chicken, chill and take to work and reheat in a microwave for 2 minutes until piping hot.

dhal soup with rice
Cook 1/4 cup brown rice, thin the dhal down with a little water. Stir in the cooked rice and serve as a thick soup.

split pea dhal
Replace the red lentils with the same quantity of yellow split peas or mung dhal, cook for slightly longer until soft.

with baked sweet potato
Bake 4 sweet potatoes in their skins until tender, split and serve with the dhal poured over.

quesadillas with whole-grain tortillas

see base recipe page 163

Italian version
Replace the cheddar with the same quantity of mozzarella, replace the cherry tomatoes with sun-dried tomatoes and the cilantro with fresh basil. Cook as before.

with black bean chili
Omit the filling and replace with a portion of the black bean chili on page 132.

with fajita filling
Omit the filling and replace with superfood fajita filling on page 161.

variations

cauliflower base pizza

see base recipe page 164

with spirulina or chlorella
This will give you a green colored base but is really good for you. Add 1 teaspoon spirulina or chlorella powder to the grated cauliflower at the same time as the parmesan.

pizza toasties
Top one of the bases with pureed tomato followed by wilted spinach, crumbled goat cheese, fresh basil, and pine nuts. Lay the other base on top, sprinkle with mozzarella, and bake for 5–10 minutes until the cheese is bubbling. Cut into wedges and serve.

mini pizzas
Divide the cauliflower base into small portions and press into mini disks to create mini pizzas or canapes. Top with a selection of your choice.

variations

roasted veg tarts with spelt cheat's puff pastry

see base recipe page 165

roasted tomato & tapenade
Replace the vegetables with a selection of different tomatoes, halved or quartered depending on their size. Roast the tomatoes as for the vegetables and cook the pastry. Spread 2 tablespoons sun-dried tomato tapenade on the pastry base, top with the roast tomatoes and sprinkle with the cheese.

roasted onion & goat cheese
Omit the vegetables, replace with 6 red onions, finely sliced and some fresh thyme. Fry the sliced onions in a skillet over a low heat for 15–20 minutes until very soft and just starting to catch at the edges. Add a tablespoon of butter and a teaspoon of coconut sugar and turn up the heat to caramelize the onions. Tip onto the pastry base, scatter with thyme leaves and the cheese and finish as in main recipe.

with mozzarella
Proceed with main recipe, replacing the feta or goat cheese with mozzarella balls.

desserts

Who knew desserts could be so delicious and good
for you? These recipes are perfect for taking care of
your body and your cravings.

raspberry tofu pudding

see variations page 220

This smooth dessert takes five minutes to prepare and is a wonderful alternative to creamy calorie-laden puddings.

4 cups raspberries
1 cup silken tofu
1/2 tsp. vanilla extract
2-3 tbsp agave, rice syrup or maple syrup

Set aside a quarter of the raspberries, place the remainder in a food processor and whizz to a puree. Press the pulp through a sieve to remove the pips.

Return the puree to the food processor with the tofu, vanilla, and syrup and blend until smooth and creamy. Serve with some of the remaining raspberries in the base of the serving dishes and the rest sprinkled on top.

Serves 3-4

banana bites with nut butter & hemp

see variations page 221

Quick and easy to make, these are an ideal dessert or a snack for adults and children alike. Vary the nuts, seeds and butters to create different flavors and textures. Bananas are a fabulous source of potassium, hemp seeds contain 10 essential amino acids, help to reduce cholesterol, and are a natural appetite suppressant.

2 firm bananas
1 tbsp. peanut butter
1 tbsp. hemp seeds
1 tbsp. black sesame seeds

Peel the bananas and cut each into 3 pieces. Spread the peanut butter over each piece, leaving around 1/2 inch so you can pick it up without getting peanut butter all over your hands and roll in hemp seeds. Serve.

Serves 2

chocolate hazelnut spread

see variations page 222

A healthier homemade version of a popular chocolate nut spread. If you wish you can buy blanched nuts and roast or leave raw, depending on which flavor you prefer.

1 cup raw hazelnuts
3–4 tbsp. raw cacao or cocoa powder
4–6 tbsp. agave, rice malt syrup, maple syrup, to taste
1/4 tsp. sea salt

2 tsp. vanilla extract
1 tbsp. coconut oil
1/2 cup, plus 2 tbsp. almond, coconut, soy or dairy milk
sourdough toast or strawberries, to serve

Preheat the oven to 430°F (220°C), place the hazelnuts on a non-stick cookie sheet and roast in the oven for 10–15 minutes. The nuts should be golden brown but not deep brown. Remove from the oven, transfer to a clean tea towel and let cool for 30 minutes.

Once cool enough to handle, rub the hazelnuts on a clean towel to loosen the skins, pick out the skinned hazelnuts, and discard the skins. Place the hazelnuts in a food processor and process until they form a paste, this may take up to 20 minutes.

Once a paste forms, add the cacao, agave, sea salt, vanilla and coconut oil. Process again to completely combine. Add the milk and process again. Taste and add more agave or salt if required. Serve with sourdough toast or drizzled on fresh strawberries.

Makes 1 jar

avocado & chocolate mousse shots

see variations page 223

Egg-free, dairy-free (use almond milk), and virtually sugar-free, this chocolate mousse tastes delicious. The avocado gives the mousse a lovely silky texture, and adds good fats, potassium, B vitamins, and folic acid. The layers of strawberries and nuts add texture and additional nutrients.

1 ripe avocado
1/4 cup milk (almond or soy for dairy-free)
2 tbsp. agave nectar
2 tbsp. raw cocoa powder
1 tsp. vanilla extract
pinch of salt

1 oz. bittersweet chocolate, melted
8 fresh strawberries
1/2 cup currants
3/4 cup hazelnuts
1/4 cup soft dates

Peel and stone the avocado, roughly chop and place in a food processor with the milk, agave, cocoa, vanilla, salt, and melted chocolate. Blend to a puree. Lightly crush the strawberries and set aside.

Put the currants, hazelnuts, and soft dates in a food processor and blend until the mixture forms a sticky mass, add a drop of agave if too crumbly. Dampen your hands to help prevent the mixture sticking and split into 8 pieces. Roll each piece into a ball and flatten to fit the width of your shot glass. Layer in shot glasses starting with the hazelnut disks, then strawberries, and finishing with the mousse. Chill and serve with extra strawberries.

Serves 4

chocolate & coconut popsicles

see variations page 224

With the inclusion of lucuma powder, raw cacao, and coconut, these popsicles are packed with nutrients. Each of the recipes can be churned in an ice cream maker to make ice cream as an to setting the mixture in popsicle molds.

Chocolate layer:
14-oz. can coconut milk
1/3 cup raw cacao powder
1/3 cup agave, rice or maple syrup
1-2 tbsp. lucuma powder
1 1/2 tbsp. coconut sugar

2 tsp. vanilla extract
pinch of salt

Coconut layer:
14-oz. can coconut milk
2 tbsp. agave, rice or maple syrup

2 tbsp. lucuma powder
1 tsp. vanilla extract
2 tsp. natural coconut flavoring
pinch of salt

In a food processor or with an immersion blender, blend together the coconut milk, cacao, syrup, and lucuma powder until well blended and thick. Pour 1/3 of the mixture into a small saucepan, add the coconut sugar and heat gently to dissolve the sugar. Once the sugar has dissolved, pour back into the chocolate coconut milk, add the vanilla and salt, and stir to mix well. For the coconut layer, repeat this process again with the coconut milk, syrup, lucuma powder, vanilla, coconut flavoring, and salt.

Place 3/4-1 1/2 inches of either the chocolate or coconut layer into a popsicle mold and freeze until almost set. Then pour the other layer over the top and freeze until set. If you want to make ice cream, churn the remaining mixtures in an ice cream maker or freeze in a freezer-proof tub, removing every hour and whisking until the mixture is solid.

Makes 12–16 popsicles

berry yogurt popsicles

see variations page 225

Homemade popsicles are a healthy treat because you can control what goes into them. They are a great way of using up extra fruit or making treats from frozen berries. Agave nectar replaces sugar and yogurt works well in place of cream.

1 cup black currants, fresh or frozen
1/2 cup blueberries, fresh or frozen
1/2 cup, plus 2 tbsp. plain yogurt
3 tbsp. agave nectar

1 tsp. acai powder
juice of 1/2 lime

Place all the ingredients in a food processor and blend to a puree, adding more lime juice if the mixture is thick.

Taste the mixture to check for sweetness as black currants can be very sour, add a little more agave if necessary. Transfer to popsicle molds and freeze for at least 8 hours or overnight.

Makes 4 popsicles

raw chocolate bars

see variations page 226

This recipe uses raw cacao, coconut oil, and a sweetener to create a deeply delicious, sugar-free, healthy alternative to chocolate. Very easy to make, the flavor of the cocoa bean comes through in the raw cacao and all of the nutrients are retained as the cacao hasn't been heat treated. The nuts and berries add additional nutrients.

2 tbsp. coconut oil
1/4 cup raw cacao powder
1 1/2 tbsp. agave or rice syrup
4 roughly chopped Brazil nuts
1 tbsp. goji berries

Melt the coconut oil until just liquid, stir in the cacao and syrup, and stir to mix. Add the nuts and berries and transfer to silicone molds or a small cookie sheet lined with baking parchment. Chill in the refrigerator for 30 minutes until set.

Makes 1 large chocolate bar

raw chocolate truffles

see variations page 227

A great way to get your chocolate fix with homemade chocolate truffles that are good for you and packed full of superfoods and nutrients. Wonderful to make as gifts for friends and family.

8 medjool dates, chopped
2 tbsp. raw cacao powder
2 tbsp. coconut oil, melted
1 tbsp. nut butter
2 tsp. maca powder

1 tsp. lucuma powder
1 tsp. acai powder
1 tbsp. agave, rice or maple syrup
shredded coconut, acai powder, cacao nibs, or
crushed nuts, for rolling

Place all the ingredients, except the shredded coconut, acai, cacao or crushed nuts, in a food processor and blend until the mixture comes together, around 3 minutes. Roll into small balls, then roll in coconut, acai, cacao nibs, or crushed nuts. Refrigerate to firm before serving.

Serves 4

no-cook raspberry cheesecake with superfood base

see variations page 228

This dessert is wonderful for family gatherings and dinner parties and beautifully light after a large meal.

3/4 cup hazelnuts or Brazil nuts
1/2 cup chia seeds
1/2 cup sunflower seeds
1/2 cup shredded coconut
2 tbsp. coconut oil or butter
2 tbsp. agave, rice or maple syrup

Filling:

3 cups cream cheese
1 cup heavy cream
3 cups fresh raspberries
3 tbsp. agave, rice or maple syrup, or raw sugar, plus a little extra

Put the nuts, seeds, and coconut in a food processor and process until well chopped. Add the oil and syrup and process briefly until the mixture comes together as a ball. Press into a greased and lined springform pan and freeze for 2 hours.

Meanwhile, whip together the cream cheese and cream until thick and able to stand in soft peaks, whip in the syrup or sugar. Gently fold in 2/3 of the raspberries, reserving the rest for the top. Put the remaining raspberries in a small saucepan with the agave or sugar and simmer gently until the berries collapse. Press through a sieve and discard the seeds. Allow the raspberry coulis to cool then chill.

Spread the cheese mixture over the base, level the top and chill for at least 2 hours or overnight. When you are ready to serve, pour over the raspberry coulis, finish with the fresh berries and carefully remove from the springform pan to serve.

Serves 8

blueberry tarts with spelt shortcrust pastry

see variations page 229

These adorable little tarts go beautifully with a cup of coffee.

2 cups spelt flour
large pinch sea salt
1/2 cup unsalted butter, diced and chilled
1/2 cup coconut sugar or raw sugar
1 egg

2 cups blueberries
zest and juice of 1 lemon
2 tbsp. chia seeds

Put the flour, salt, and diced butter in a food processor and process until it resembles breadcrumbs. Add half the sugar and pulse quickly to blend. Add the egg and blend to bring it to a dough. Transfer to a freezer bag and chill for an hour.

Put half the blueberries in a small saucepan over a low heat, add the lemon zest and juice and the rest of the sugar. Cook for 5 minutes until the fruit begins to collapse. Meanwhile, soak the chia seeds in 8 tablespoons of water and leave for 5–10 minutes until thick and gel-like. Stir the chia seeds into the blueberry mixture along with the remaining blueberries.

Preheat the oven to 400°F (200°C). Grease 4 mini loose-bottomed tart tins, line with the pastry, place a sheet of baking parchment in the center of the pastry, tip in baking beans and bake blind for 10–15 minutes until golden brown. Leave until completely cold. When cold, divide the blueberry mixture between the cases and chill for at least an hour to allow the fruit to settle.

Serves 4

apple & raw chocolate bites

see variations page 230

Ideal snacks, these are easy to pack and eat on the go.

2 eating apples
1 quantity of raw chocolate
    (see page 201 for recipe)
1 tbsp. each chopped pecans,
    goji berries, and chia seeds,
    mixed together

Cut the eating apples into quarters and remove the core. Cut each quarter into 3 wedges.

Melt the raw chocolate. Have a piece of baking parchment ready.

Dip each apple wedge into the chocolate and then sprinkle with the chopped nuts, berries and chia seeds, lay on the parchment and repeat with the rest of the apple wedges.

Chill in the refrigerator until ready to eat.

Serves 4

rainbow superfood popsicles

see variations page 231

Summer treats that kids and teens will love.

1/2 cup strawberries
agave, rice syrup, or maple syrup to taste
2 limes, juice and zest
1 mango
1 tsp. lucuma powder

3 kiwi fruit
1/2 tsp. spirulina or chlorella powder
3/4 cup black currants
1 tsp. acai powder

Hull and chop the strawberries, blend to a puree, adding a little syrup and a squeeze of lime to taste. Pour into popsicle molds and freeze for 30 minutes to 1 hour until firm. Leave sufficient room in the mold to add the other colors.

Peel and dice the mango, removing the pit, puree with the lucuma powder and add a little syrup if required, it may be sweet enough on its own. Pour on top of the frozen strawberry layer, freeze until firm.

Peel and chop the kiwi fruit, add the spirulina or chlorella powder, the juice and zest of a lime, puree, taste and add a little syrup if necessary. Pour on top of the frozen mango layer, freeze until firm.

Puree the black currants, add the acai powder, plus a little syrup to taste. Sieve to remove the seeds, pour into the mold as the final layer. Freeze until firm.

Makes 10 popsicles

superfruit crumble

see variations page 232

A superfood take on classic crumble, serve with a dollop of Greek yogurt mixed with a little cinnamon and vanilla extract.

1/2 cup whole-grain all-purpose flour
3 tbsp. butter, cubed, or coconut oil
1/3 cup coconut sugar
1 cup rolled oats
1/2 cup slivered almonds
1/4 cup Brazil nuts, chopped
1/4 cup walnuts, chopped

1/2 tsp. ground cinnamon
4 plums, quartered, pits removed
1 cup blueberries
2 tbsp. coconut sugar or 2–3 tbsp. agave
   or rice syrup
1 tsp. ground ginger

Preheat the oven to 350°F (180°C). Rub the butter or coconut oil into the flour with your fingertips until it resembles breadcrumbs, or pulse in a food processor. Stir in the coconut sugar, rolled oats, nuts, and cinnamon.

Mix the plums and blueberries together, divide between 4 ramekins or place in an ovenproof dish, sprinkle with coconut sugar and ginger.

Sprinkle over the crumble topping and bake for 20–30 minutes until the fruit is bubbling and the topping is golden brown and serve.

Serves 4

roasted peaches & plums with ricotta cream

see variations page 233

The fruit can be served warm and makes a lovely dessert for chilly autumn or winter evenings or chilled and eaten on hot summer days. The ricotta cream is a healthy alternative to cream.

1 cup ricotta
1 tbsp. agave or maple syrup
4 pieces of preserved ginger, drained and finely chopped
1 tsp. ground cinnamon
2 tbsp. toasted pine nuts

2 ripe peaches or nectarines
4 plums
4 apricots
1 tbsp. each sunflower oil and agave mixed together

Begin the day before. Mix together the ricotta and agave or maple syrup, beat well. Line a sieve with a large piece of muslin or a clean towel and pour in the ricotta. Secure the top and lay the sieve over a bowl. Lay a plate on top and weigh down with something heavy. Refrigerate overnight. This will make the ricotta crumblier in texture. The next day mix in the finely chopped preserved ginger, cinnamon, and pine nuts. Chill until ready.

Preheat the oven to 375°F (190°C). Halve the fruit and remove the pits. Brush with the sunflower oil and agave, place in a greased casserole dish and roast for 8–10 minutes until soft and slightly caramelized. Serve warm or cold with the chilled ricotta cream spooned over the top.

Serves 4

raw instant ice cream

see variations page 234

So simple, quick and delicious you'll wonder why you haven't been making this for years. This is a great way of using very ripe bananas, just peel, chop, and freeze them in bags ready for use. You will need to begin the day before unless you have bananas in the freezer already, they need to be frozen to work. Also be prepared to serve it immediately, you can't refreeze it and if it's a hot day it will defrost very quickly.

3 very ripe bananas, peeled, chopped in 4–6 chunky slices and frozen
1–2 tsp. vanilla extract
goji berries and strawberry slices, or acai powder, to serve

Put the frozen banana slices in a food processor and process for a couple of minutes until the mixture becomes smooth, keep scraping down any banana pieces that become caught at the edges.

Add 1 teaspoon vanilla, mix quickly and taste, add another if you wish.

Transfer to bowls, sprinkle over some goji berries, strawberries, or a sprinkling of acai powder, serve and eat straightaway.

Serves 2

matcha green tea ice cream

see variations page 235

Mild and refreshing in flavor and ever so good for you, serve with a selection of tropical sliced fruit.

3 egg yolks
1/2 cup superfine sugar
1 tsp. matcha green tea powder
2 cups, plus 1 tbsp. whole milk
1/2 cup heavy cream

In a standing mixer, whisk the egg yolks and superfine sugar together until the mixture turns pale yellow and leaves a "trail" when the beater is pulled out of the mix. Whisk in the green tea powder until smooth and there are no lumps.

Heat the milk in a saucepan until it just comes to a boil. Remove the saucepan from the heat and plunge it into a sink of cold water for 10 minutes to cool the milk down. Stir in the egg yolk mixture and return to a low heat, stirring constantly for around 10 minutes until the mixture thickens sufficiently to "coat" the back of a wooden spoon. Then stir in the cream. Do not allow it to boil, if it does the mixture will curdle and to bring it back you will need to plunge the saucepan into cold water and whisk vigorously for 10 minutes or until it becomes smooth again.

Chill overnight and churn in an ice cream maker. Transfer to the freezer and freeze until solid.

Serves 4

raspberry frozen greek yogurt

see variations page 236

Sweet and tangy, this is a fabulous dessert for the summer and goes particularly well with a drizzle of runny honey.

3 1/2 cups fresh raspberries
1 1/4 cups Greek yogurt
3–4 tbsp. agave or honey

Press the raspberries through a sieve to extract a puree, the puree should come to around 1/2 cup, don't worry if it's not exact.

Whisk the raspberry puree with the Greek yogurt and agave, this will turn the mixture a lovely deep pink and loosen up the yogurt.

Churn in an ice cream maker until almost frozen then transfer to a freezer-safe container and freeze until ready to use. Defrost for 30-40 minutes before serving to allow time to soften up.

Serves 4

chocolate & nut almond milk ice cream

see variations page 237

This sumptuous ice cream is high in protein and antioxidants making it the healthiest chocolate dessert you've ever had.

3 egg yolks
1/2 cup superfine sugar
3 1/4 cups, plus 1 tbsp. almond milk
2 tbsp. raw cacao powder

1 tsp. vanilla extract
pinch xanthan gum
1/3 cup hazelnuts, lightly toasted and chopped

In a stand mixer whisk the egg yolks and superfine sugar together until the mixture turns pale yellow and leaves a "trail" when the beater is lifted out of the mix.

Heat the milk in a saucepan, whisk in the cacao powder, and cook over a low heat until it just comes to a boil. Remove the saucepan from the heat and plunge into a sink of cold water for 10 minutes to cool the milk down. Stir half the milk mixture into the egg yolk mixture, tip the mixture back into the saucepan and stir to mix in the rest of the mixture. Stir in the vanilla and xanthan gum. Return to a low heat, stirring constantly for around a few minutes until the mixture thickens sufficiently to "coat" the back of a wooden spoon. Do not allow it to boil, if it does the mixture will curdle and to bring it back you will need to plunge the saucepan into cold water and whisk vigorously for 10 minutes or until it becomes smooth again. Chill overnight and churn in an ice cream maker. Stir in the chopped nuts and transfer to the freezer and freeze until solid.

Serves 4

raspberry tofu pudding

see base recipe page 193

mango tofu pudding
Replace the raspberries with the flesh of 1 large ripe mango.

strawberry tofu pudding
Replace the raspberries with the same quantity of strawberries and a teaspoon of balsamic vinegar.

blueberry tofu pudding
Replace the raspberries with the same quantity of blueberries.

chocolate tofu pudding
Replace the raspberries with 4 ounces bittersweet chocolate, melted and blend with the tofu as before.

banana bites with nut butter & hemp

see base recipe page 194

with homemade hazelnut spread & hazelnuts
Replace the peanut butter with homemade hazelnut spread (see page 196) and the hemp seeds with toasted chopped hazelnuts.

with almond butter & sesame
Replace the peanut butter with homemade cashew nut butter (see page 240) and the hemp seeds with toasted sesame seeds.

with chocolate, coconut & pistachio
Omit the peanut butter and hemp seeds. Melt a little bittersweet chocolate, dunk the banana pieces into the chocolate, then into toasted shredded coconut and finally in some chopped pistachios.

with homemade hazelnut spread, acai & goji berries
Replace the peanut butter with homemade hazelnut spread (see page 196) and the hemp seeds with goji berries, dust with acai powder.

variations

chocolate hazelnut spread

see base recipe page 196

chocolate chile hazelnut spread
Add 1 finely diced red chile at the same time as the cacao powder.

chocolate roasted nut spread
Replace the hazelnuts with 1 cup mixed nuts, proceed with main recipe.

nut-free chocolate spread
For those of you with nut allergies replace the hazelnuts with 2 1/2 cups sunflower seeds, do not roast, just process as in main recipe.

more authentic but not quite as healthy version
Omit the cacao powder and replace with 2 cups milk chocolate and 1 cup bittersweet chocolate melted together. Replace the agave with 1/4 cup coconut sugar or superfine sugar.

avocado & chocolate mousse shots

see base recipe page 197

chile chocolate & avocado mousse
Add one finely chopped and deseeded fresh red chile to the mousse mixture once it's been blended to a puree.

raspberry chocolate & avocado mousse
Omit the strawberries and nut mixture. Lightly crush 1 cup fresh raspberries and layer between the mousse, top with a few chopped Brazil nuts.

chocolate orange & avocado mousse
Omit the strawberries and nut mixture. Grate the zest of 2 oranges into the mousse mixture and blend to a puree. Serve with segments of orange or clementine.

chocolate banana & avocado mousse
Omit the strawberries and nut mixture. Slice a banana and layer the slices of banana with the mousse and finely chopped pistachios to create a wonderful stripy effect, finish with a few goji berries sprinkled on top.

variations

chocolate & coconut popsicles

see base recipe page 199

chocolate beet popsicles
Omit the coconut layer, stir in 1 large peeled and finely grated beet to the chocolate mixture and fill popsicle molds.

chocolate orange popsicles
Omit the coconut layer, add the grated zest of 2 large oranges to the chocolate mixture and fill popsicle molds.

chocolate mint popsicles
Omit the coconut layer, add a handful of finely chopped fresh mint and 2 teaspoons natural mint flavoring to the chocolate mixture and fill popsicle molds.

with instant chocolate shell
Melt 1 1/2 tablespoons coconut oil with 1/2 cup bittersweet chocolate chips over a double boiler, mix well and pour over the set popsicles.

with instant chocolate shell & toasted coconut
Make the instant chocolate shell as above, toast 1/2 cup shredded coconut in a dry skillet until golden and aromatic, let cool. Dunk the popsicles into the shell and immediately into the toasted coconut, eat right away.

berry yogurt popsicles

see base recipe page 200

creamy berry yogurt popsicles

Add a scant 1 cup coconut milk to the mixture at the end, do not mix it, just gently swirl it around to achieve a mottled effect. This will reduce the tartness of the black currants and increase the yield to 6–7 popsicles. If you run out of popsicle molds, fill ice cube trays for mini versions and use toothpicks for popsicle sticks, take care with the points though.

strawberry yogurt popsicles

Replace the black currants and blueberries with 2 cups fresh, hulled, and chopped strawberries, reduce the agave nectar to 1 tablespoon and add 1 tablespoon balsamic vinegar, check for sweetness. Make a creamy version by adding the coconut milk and proceeding with main recipe.

raspberry & chocolate yogurt popsicles

Replace the black currants and blueberries with 2 cups fresh raspberries, reduce the agave nectar to 1 tablespoon and mix 1 cup melted bittersweet chocolate with a scant 1 cup coconut cream. Pour the raspberry mixture half way up the popsicles molds then pour in the chocolate so they mix slightly. This will make up to 8 popsicles.

raw chocolate bars

see base recipe page 201

with crushed pistachios
Replace the Brazil nuts with 1 tablespoon crushed pistachios.

with freeze dried raspberries
Replace the goji berries with the same quantity of freeze dried raspberry pieces.

with roast hazelnuts & flame raisins
Replace the Brazil nuts with the same quantity of lightly roasted, roughly chopped hazelnuts and the goji berries with the same quantity of flame raisins.

with pecans & cranberries
Replace the Brazil nuts with the same quantity of roughly chopped pecans and the goji berries with the same quantity of dried cranberries.

with sweetener
For a lower calorie version replace the syrup with 1–2 teaspoons stevia syrup, taste and add more if required.

variations

raw chocolate truffles

see base recipe page 202

raw chocolate shell
Make up a quantity of the raw chocolate (see page 201), refrigerate the chocolate truffles for an hour, remove from the refrigerator and dunk into the raw chocolate. Lay on a sheet of baking parchment and refrigerate to harden.

peanut butter & chocolate shell
Flatten the balls slightly, spread with a layer of crunchy peanut butter and dunk into the raw chocolate shell, lay on a sheet of baking parchment and refrigerate to harden.

chile version
Add 1 finely chopped, deseeded red chile to the mixture after it's been processed.

cardamom version
Remove the seeds from 6 cardamom pods and crush the seeds in a pestle and mortar, add the ground cardamom to the mixture at the same time as the acai.

variations

no-cook raspberry cheesecake with superfood base

see base recipe page 204

white chocolate & raspberry

Melt 2 cups chopped white chocolate with 3 1/2 tablespoons butter and 1/2 teaspoon vanilla extract. Reduce the cream cheese to 1 1/2 cups and the cream to 1/2 cup. Whip the cream cheese and cream, then stir in the melted chocolate and butter and proceed with main recipe.

chocolate & raspberry

Replace the white chocolate with bittersweet chocolate and proceed with recipe for white chocolate & raspberry cheesecake above.

strawberry swirl

Replace the raspberries with the same quantity of strawberries. Reserve 1 cup strawberries and chop the remaining 2 cups. Place in a saucepan with a little syrup and heat until the berries collapse, press through a sieve and cool. Mix the cream cheese filling then swirl through the coulis. Slice remaining strawberries to decorate.

blueberry & acai

Replace the raspberries with the same quantity of blueberries and proceed with main recipe, adding 1 tablespoon acai powder to the cream cheese mixture.

blueberry tarts with spelt shortcrust pastry

see base recipe page 206

pumpkin pie
Omit the filling and replace with a 14-oz can of pumpkin puree, 1 egg,
1 tablespoon maple syrup, 1 teaspoon of ground cinnamon, 1/2 teaspoon
ground ginger, grated zest of 1 orange and a little almond milk. Mix
together to form a thick filling. Pour into the cooked tart cases and reduce
the oven to 350°F (180°C) and bake for 10 minutes until the filling is firm
and springy to the touch.

plum & berry
Replace the blueberries with 1 cup chopped plums and 1 cup raspberries.
Cook the fruit gently in a saucepan with the coconut sugar as before, add
the chia seeds and proceed with main recipe.

pear & frangipane
Omit the filling, cream 1/2 cup soft butter with 1/2 cup superfine sugar,
add 3 medium eggs and 3/4 cup almond meal with the zest of a lemon and
share between the cooked pastry cases. Peel, core and quarter a ripe pear,
thinly slice each quarter and place over the frangipane in each of the tart
cases. Bake for 10–15 minutes until the filling is golden brown and springy
to the touch.

variations

apple & raw chocolate bites

see base recipe page 207

with chopped brazil nuts & cranberries
Replace the pecans and goji berries with the same quantity of Brazil nuts and cranberries.

with chopped pistachios
Replace the pecans, goji berries, and chia seeds with 1 tablespoon chopped pistachios.

with freeze fried raspberries
Replace the pecans, goji berries, and chia seeds with 1 tablespoon freeze dried raspberries.

with black sesame seeds
Replace the pecans, goji berries, and chia seeds with the same quantity of black sesame seeds.

rainbow superfood popsicles

see base recipe page 209

raspberry & blueberry version
Omit the fruit, replace with 2 cups raspberries and 2 cups blueberries, leaving 20 whole, and puree each fruit adding 2 teaspoons acai to the blueberries and syrup, if required. Layer red, then blue, red, blue. Add 2 blueberries to the final red layer in the popsicles mold so they can be seen through the red.

pineapple & passion fruit version
If your popsicle molds are sufficiently long you could add 1/2 pineapple, peeled, chopped and pureed with the seeds of a passion fruit stirred into the puree as an extra layer between the mango and kiwi.

full rainbow effect popsicles
Add additional layers for a full rainbow effect such as strawberry, mango, pineapple/passion fruit, kiwi, blueberry, and black currant.

variations

superfruit crumble

see base recipe page 210

with coconut & pecans
Add 1/2 cup shredded coconut or coconut flakes to the crumble and replace the walnuts with the same quantity of pecans.

gluten-free
Replace the flour with buckwheat or other gluten-free flour. Use gluten-free oats.

chocolate crumble
Add 2 tablespoons raw cacao powder to the crumble topping at the same time as the oats and increase the cinnamon to 1 teaspoon.

roasted peaches & plums with ricotta cream

see base recipe page 213

fresh berries & ricotta cream

This is lovely taken on a picnic, use a selection of berries such as strawberries, blueberries, and raspberries as well as peaches, plums, and apricots. Serve the fruit whole if small enough or in wedges and use the ricotta cream as a dip.

almond-stuffed fruit

Make up the ricotta cream as in main recipe, halve fruit such as a combination of peaches, nectarines, plums, mango, or apples and remove the pit. Combine 3/4 cup almond meal, 1 tablespoon raw cacao, 1 tablespoon coconut sugar and 1 1/2 tablespoons softened unsalted butter to make a stiff paste. Stuff the center of the fruit with the paste and roast at 350°F (180°C) for 10–15 minutes until the fruit is soft. Serve with the ricotta cream on the side.

granola fruit layer

Make the granola on page 25, layer the roasted fruit with granola and ricotta cream in a tall sundae dish and drizzle with a little black currant or raspberry coulis.

variations

raw instant ice cream

see base recipe page 214

strawberry & banana ice cream
Reduce to 2 bananas, add 8 chopped, frozen strawberries and process as in main recipe, add 1 teaspoon balsamic vinegar.

acai ice cream
Stir in 1 tablespoon acai powder to the banana just before serving, you could swirl it in for a marbled purple effect. Acai has very little flavor but is rich in nutrients and antioxidants.

black currant & blueberry ice cream
Replace 1 banana with 1/2 cup frozen blueberries and 1/2 cup frozen black currants plus 1 tablespoon acai powder, process until smooth, drizzle with a little agave, honey or maple syrup if a little sour.

chocolate banana ice cream
Make as before, stir in 1 tablespoon raw cacao powder and 1 tablespoon raw chocolate chips just before serving for a healthy chocolate ice cream.

creamy raw ice cream
Add 1 tablespoon thick coconut cream to the mix when processing, this makes the ice cream extra smooth without tasting of coconut.

matcha green tea ice cream

see base recipe page 215

with chocolate chips
Add 1/2 cup bittersweet chocolate chips to the ice cream once it has been churned and before transferring to the freezer.

with blueberry coulis
Gently heat 1 1/2 cups blueberries with 2 tablespoons agave or rice syrup in a saucepan for 5–10 minutes until the fruit collapses, press through a sieve and drizzle over the ice cream.

with granola
Serve with a sprinkling of granola on top (see page 25) and some fresh fruit.

with vanilla & mint
Add 1 teaspoon vanilla extract and 1 bunch of chopped fresh mint leaves to the mixture just before churning, serve with chopped toasted nuts and fresh berries.

with olive oil & sea salt
Sounds odd but tastes fabulous, serve with a drizzle of fruity extra virgin olive oil and a sprinkle of sea salt.

raspberry frozen greek yogurt

see base recipe page 217

with chocolate chips
Add 1/2 cup bittersweet chocolate chips or chopped chocolate to the mix before transferring to the freezer.

with magic chocolate sauce
Melt 1/2 cup coconut oil and 1 cup raw bittersweet chocolate, pour over the ice cream and it will instantly set to form a shell.

chocolate frozen yogurt with raspberries
Omit the raspberries. Melt 1 cup raw bittersweet chocolate with 3 tablespoons agave and 1/2 cup plus 2 tablespoons almond milk over a low heat. Let cool completely and chill before using. Add 2 tablespoons raw cacao powder and whisk in the Greek yogurt, check sweetness and churn. Stir in 2 cups raspberries before transferring to freezer.

orange & honey
Omit the raspberries, add the juice and zest of 3 oranges and proceed with main recipe.

with brownie pieces
Make the black bean brownies on page 248, cut half the batch into small 1/2-inch square pieces then stir into the raspberry yogurt before transferring to the freezer.

variations

chocolate & nut almond milk ice cream

see base recipe page 218

vanilla version
Omit the cacao powder and hazelnuts and add an additional teaspoon of vanilla extract. Proceed with main recipe.

strawberry version
Puree 2 cups strawberries in a food processor, press through a sieve to remove the seeds and stir into the chilled mixture, proceed with main recipe.

mint choc chip version
Omit the cacao powder and vanilla extract, replace with 2 teaspoons natural peppermint extract and stir in 1/2 cup bittersweet chocolate chips before freezing.

baking

Eating healthily doesn't mean you have to give up wonderful baked goods. This chapter gives you some comforting, beneficial recipes to indulge that sweet tooth.

raw raspberry chia jelly

see variations page 265

We all love jelly but usually most of the nutrients have been cooked out of the sugary mixture. This recipe requires no cooking so most of the nutrients are preserved. I've added agave for sweetness but you can change this for honey, maple syrup, or stevia, and be careful to avoid overpowering the fruit with sweetness. Chia seeds give the jelly texture and add omega 3 fats, fiber, and help to stabilize your blood sugar and lower cholesterol.

2 cups fresh raspberries
1 tbsp. chia seeds, rinsed
1 tbsp. agave, honey or maple syrup

Wash the raspberries and blend in a food processor. Transfer to a clean, screw top jar with plenty of room for the mixture to "grow" or expand upward and stir in the chia seeds and agave.

Cover, refrigerate, and leave overnight. In the morning your jelly will have increased in volume and be thick as the chia seeds will have expanded.

Serve on oatmeal, toasted sourdough bread, pancakes, or homemade scones.

Keep refrigerated and use within 3 days.

Makes 1 jar

cashew nut butter

see variations page 266

Homemade nut butter is such a simple recipe to make, the resulting butter is made purely of nuts and you can vary all the recipes by roasting the nuts before pureeing.

1 1/2 cups cashew nuts

Place the nuts in a food processor and process. It will take around 10-15 minutes and will seem like the nuts are only being chopped but be patient.

Stop the processor occasionally and scrape the nuts from the sides then continue, eventually the nuts will clump together. Keep processing until the mixture becomes creamy. Stop the machine when the nut butter has reached the consistency you prefer; keep going for very smooth butter, stop sooner if you prefer coarse butter.

Transfer to a clean, sterilized, screw top jar and store in the refrigerator for up to 3 weeks.

Makes 1 small jar butter

raw carrot & orange cake

see variations page 267

This cake retains all the goodness in the nuts and carrots as they are not cooked, it has the texture of a passion cake and is completely delicious. The main issue is not eating all of it in one go, which is why it is great to make and share with friends.

3 medium carrots
2 cups walnut pieces
1/2 cup toasted hazelnut
    pieces
3/4 cup raisins
1 tbsp. sunflower seeds
1 tbsp. pumpkin seeds
1 tbsp. chia seeds

1 tbsp. flaxseeds
2 tbsp. agave, maple syrup or
    honey
1 tsp. vanilla extract
2 tsp. ground cinnamon
zest of 1 orange
a little water

Cashew frosting:
1 cup cashew nuts
2 tbsp. freshly squeezed
    orange juice
2 tbsp. agave, maple syrup or
    honey
1 tsp. vanilla extra
a little water

Put the carrots in a food processor and pulse until they become small chunks, add the rest of the cake ingredients and process in short bursts until you have a crumbly "carrot" cake texture. Do not over process, it needs to be lumpy, not smooth. You should be able to see the different colors of the carrots, pumpkin seeds and nuts in the mixture. Transfer to a lined square cake pan or muffin cases and press mixture down.

To make the frosting, put all the ingredients in the food processor and pulse until smooth, adding a little extra water or juice if it's too stiff. Ice the cake and refrigerate for 3–4 hours or overnight before serving to ensure that the cake and frosting have time to solidify. Slice and serve.

Makes 8–12

carrot muffins

see variations page 268

The carrots, cinnamon, and whole-grain flour help to turn these muffins into a healthier version of the classic.

1 cup self-rising flour
3/4 cup whole-grain self-
rising flour
1/2 cup light muscovado
sugar
1/2 tsp. baking powder
pinch of salt
1 tsp. ground cinnamon

1/2 cup, plus 2 tbsp. coconut
or sunflower oil
2 large eggs
1/2 cup almond, dairy, or
soy milk
2 medium carrots, grated

Frosting:
3 1/2 tbsp. soft butter
1/3 cup cream cheese
2 cups confectioners' sugar
grated zest of 1 orange
a little orange juice
fondant carrots, to serve

Preheat the oven to 400°F (200°C). Place a shelf in the center.

Mix together the flours, muscovado sugar, baking powder, salt, and cinnamon.

Mix the oil with the eggs and milk, beat lightly, and add to the dry ingredients, mix well. Add the carrots and mix everything well. Divide the mixture evenly between 12 muffin cases in a muffin pan. Bake for 15–20 minutes until they are pale golden brown. Transfer to a wire rack to cool.

To make the cream cheese frosting, cream the butter and cream cheese together, beat in the confectioners' sugar and orange zest with a little orange juice to create a soft but not runny frosting. Frost the muffins and serve topped with fondant carrots.

Makes 12 muffins

freeform plum tart with sweet almond pastry

see variations page 269

This recipe is super simple to prepare and makes a beautiful rustic dessert that is allergy friendly.

2 cups almond meal
1/2 cup almond flour
2 tbsp. lucuma powder
3 tbsp. rice syrup, agave or honey
1 tbsp. coconut oil
large pinch sea salt

2 tsp. vanilla extract
1 large egg, plus extra for egg wash
4 cups plums, pits removed and quartered
coconut sugar, to sprinkle

Combine the almonds, flour, and lucuma powder, stir in the syrup, coconut oil, salt, vanilla, and egg and bring together to form a dough. Transfer to a freezer bag and chill in the refrigerator for 1 hour before using.

Preheat the oven to 400°F (200°C). Grease and line a cookie sheet. Roll the dough into a ball and press into a round shape on the baking parchment. Pile the plum pieces onto the pastry round, pull up the edges to hold the fruit in place, brush the edges with egg and sprinkle with coconut sugar. Bake for 15–20 minutes until golden brown.

Serves 6

black bean brownies

see variations page 270

High in protein, low-carb, and gluten-free.

14-oz. can black beans, drained and rinsed
3 eggs
3 tbsp. butter or coconut oil, melted
2–3 tbsp. raw cacao powder
2 tsp. vanilla extract

1/3 cup agave nectar or 1/2 cup coconut or
    superfine sugar (if using superfine sugar,
    melt with the butter or oil)
1/2 cup walnuts, chopped
1/2 cup raw chocolate chips

Preheat the oven to 350°F (180°C).

Put all the ingredients except the walnuts and chocolate chips in a food processor and blend until smooth. Stir in the walnuts and sprinkle over the chocolate chips.

Grease and line an 8-inch (20-cm.) square cake pan, pour in the mixture and bake for 20–25 minutes until the center is firm to the touch.

Allow to cool before slicing.

Serves 9

sweet potato & orange cupcakes

see variations page 271

Orange-fleshed sweet potatoes are rich in beta carotene (a source of vitamin A), and eating fat with beta carotene rich foods helps the body absorb vitamins, so using them as an ingredient in cupcakes works well.

2 medium sweet potatoes
1/2 cup soft butter
1 cup light muscovado sugar
3 large eggs
1 3/4 cups whole-grain self-
    rising flour

1/2 tsp. baking powder
1/4 tsp. salt
1 tsp. ground cinnamon
1 tsp. ground ginger
1/2 tsp. mixed spice
pinch ground nutmeg

1/2 tsp. vanilla
finely grated zest of 1 orange
1 3/4 cups confectioners'
    sugar
juice and finely grated zest of
    1–2 oranges

To cook the sweet potatoes, bake in a hot oven, in their skins for 40–45 minutes, until soft. Split and scoop out the flesh. Do not boil the potatoes as they soak up water and your mix may not rise properly. Preheat the oven to 350°F (180°C).

Cream the butter and sugar together until light and fluffy, add the mashed sweet potato and beat. Beat the eggs, add to the mixture. Sieve in the flour, baking powder, salt and spices, fold into the mixture, add the vanilla and orange zest and gently mix together. Divide between 12 muffin cases in a muffin tray. Bake for 20–25 minutes until golden brown and firm to the touch. Cool on cooling rack. Sieve the confectioners' sugar into a bowl, add sufficient juice to mix to a stiff paste then ice the cakes. Decorate with orange zest.

Makes 12 cupcakes

kale cupcakes with cream cheese frosting

see variations page 272

These are super-cool orange-flavored green cupcakes. They still contain the same calories, sugar, and fat as a standard cupcake but the addition of the kale gives them extra nutrients and makes them ever so slightly healthier.

3 cups kale, leaves only, stalks removed
3/4 cup soft butter or margarine
3/4 cup superfine sugar
3 eggs
1 1/4 cups self-rising flour
zest of 2 oranges

Cream cheese frosting:
3 1/2 tbsp. soft butter
1/3 cup cream cheese
3 cups confectioners' sugar, sieved
zest of 1 orange, plus extra for decorating
a little freshly squeezed orange juice

Preheat the oven on to 350°F (180°C). Steam the kale for 3–4 minutes until tender, drain, rinse in cold water and squeeze gently to remove as much water as possible. Put in a food processor and briefly pulse so that the kale is finely shredded but not liquidized.

Cream the butter and sugar until pale and fluffy. Add the eggs and flour and mix well, gently fold in the orange zest and kale. Split the mixture between 12 cupcake cups in a muffin pan and bake for 20–25 minutes until golden brown and springy to the touch. Transfer to a cooling rack, and cool completely before frosting. To make the frosting, beat the butter and cream cheese until very soft, add the remaining ingredients, then beat well to achieve a soft frosting. Frost the cupcakes and sprinkle with a little more orange zest to serve.

Makes 12 cupcakes

spelt & seed bread

see variations page 273

Compared to wheat flour, spelt is richer in many nutrients and minerals, and makes a very tasty bread.

4 cups whole-grain spelt flour
1/2 cup sunflower seeds
1 tbsp. linseed
2 tbsp. pumpkin seeds

1 tsp. sea salt
2 tsp. fresh yeast or 1 tsp. dried yeast
1 1/2 cups warm water
a little olive oil

Mix together the flour, seeds, and salt. Sprinkle the yeast into the water and stir (if using dried yeast this can be mixed with the flour). Make a well in the center of the flour and tip in the water. Use a wooden spoon and mix together until a sticky dough forms.

Transfer the dough to a clean, oiled bowl, cover with plastic wrap and set aside in a warm place. After 15 minutes uncover the dough, gently pull the outside of the dough into the center, turning the bowl and continuing all the way around, probably around 8-10 "pulls". Repeat this process with 15 minute intervals another 3 times, then leave the dough to double in size for 1 hour.

Next, lightly flour a board and gently tip the dough onto it. Oil a bread pan, around 8 x 4-in. (20 x 10 cm.) fold in the outside edges of the dough to the middle and repeat-with the other edges to form an oblong shape. Place this gently into the bread pan, cover with oiled plastic wrap and leave for 45 minutes until almost doubled in size. Preheat the oven to its highest setting. When the dough has almost doubled reduce the temperature to 430°F (220°C) and bake for 20-30 minutes until golden brown and the base when tapped sounds hollow.

Makes 1 loaf

kamut bread

see variations page 274

Probably the easiest bread in the world to make, no kneading at all required.

4 cups kamut flour
1 tsp. salt
1 1/2 cups warm water

2 tsp. fresh yeast or 1 tsp. dried yeast
2 tbsp. extra virgin olive oil

Mix the flour and salt together. In a separate bowl whisk together the warm water and fresh or dried yeast. Once dissolved add the olive oil.

Make a well in the center of the flour, pour in the water and yeast mixture and mix with a wooden spoon. Once it's almost mixed use your hands to bring it all together—do not add more flour, if your hands stick dip your fingers in a little olive oil. Mix the dough well with your hands until it is smooth, be gentle, there is no need to "knead" it in the traditional way.

Lightly oil a clean bowl and transfer the dough to the bowl, cover with plastic wrap and leave in a warm place for an hour. Lightly oil a 8 x 4-in. (20 x 10-cm.) loaf tin, fold the dough into the center and repeat with the other edges to form an oblong and put with fold down in the loaf pan. Cover with oiled plastic wrap and leave for 30 minutes to prove.

Preheat the oven to 430°F (220°C) and bake the loaf for 20-25 minutes until golden brown and when you tap on the bottom it sounds hollow. Let cool and eat.

Makes 1 loaf

superfood crackers

see variations page 275

These go beautifully with cheese.

1 3/4 cups spelt flour
2 tbsp. olive oil
3 1/2 tbsp. butter, softened
1 tbsp. chia seeds
1/4 cup sunflower seeds
2 tbsp. pumpkin seeds, pulsed quickly in a food
    processor

1 tbsp. black sesame seeds
1 tbsp. alfalfa seeds
1/2 tsp. sweet paprika
1/2 tsp. salt
1 tbsp. agave nectar or honey
1/4–1/3 cup water

Preheat the oven to 350°F (180°C). Put all the ingredients in a food processor, and mix well to form a dough, adding sufficient water to hold the mixture together. Once it has come together, use your hands to press it into a ball and work the dough for 1–2 minutes to make sure it stays together.

Roll the dough out gently to 1/8 inch thickness between 2 sheets of baking parchment, cut into squares or oblongs, transfer to a greased and lined cookie sheet. Bake for 10–15 minutes until golden brown and crispy.

Makes 12–16 crackers

blackberry & apple flapjack

see variations page 276

This flapjack is sticky and moist. With the addition of fresh fruit it is wise to store it in the refrigerator to prevent it spoiling.

1/2 cup butter
1/3 cup demerara sugar
2 tbsp. maple syrup, agave syrup
    or rice syrup
1 cup rolled oats
1 cup jumbo rolled oats

1/2 cup sunflower seeds
1/4 cup pumpkin seeds
1/3 cup Brazil nuts, chopped
1 large Granny Smith apple, peeled and grated
2 cups blackberries, washed

Preheat the oven to 350°F (180°C).

Melt the butter, sugar, and syrup over a low heat. Remove from the heat and add the oats, seeds and nuts, stir to mix. Gently stir in the grated apple.

Grease and line a 9-inch (23-cm.) square cake pan with baking parchment. Press half the flapjack mixture into the base of the pan. Mash the blackberries with a fork and spread these on top of the flapjack mixture, top with the rest of the flapjack mixture, leaving the blackberries sandwiched in the middle.

Bake in the center of the oven for 20–25 minutes until nicely browned. Cut into squares and leave in the pan to cool completely.

Makes 12 flapjacks

granola bars

see variations page 277

Healthy food on the go, don't leave home without these. This version gives a soft, chewy bar, if you prefer crunchy bars try some of the variations.

4 cups granola (see page 25)
3 tsp. acai powder
2 tsp. maca powder
3 small ripe bananas
1/2 cup nut butter

Preheat the oven to 375°F (190°C). Grease and line a 9-inch (23-cm.) square cake pan.

Mix the granola with the acai and maca powder. Mash the bananas and beat in the nut butter until the mixture is smooth.

Add to the granola and mix well to combine, pour into the prepared cake pan, press down well with your fingers, and bake for 10–15 minutes until golden brown.

Cut into squares and cool in the pan. Store in an airtight container.

Makes 12 bars

date & walnut cake

see variations page 278

Sweet and indulgent, ideal served with coffee.

1 cup dates, chopped and
   pitted
1 cup boiling water
1 tsp. baking soda
2 tbsp. butter, diced
3/4 cup spelt flour
1 cup whole-grain flour
2 tsp. baking powder
1 tsp. mixed spice
1 tsp. ground cinnamon
large pinch ground cloves

1 tbsp. lucuma powder
1/2 tsp. freshly grated nutmeg
1/2 tsp. ground ginger
1 large egg
3/4 cup dark muscovado
   sugar
1 tsp. vanilla extract
1 cup walnuts, roughly
   chopped
1/2 cup almond meal

Raw walnut frosting:
1 cup walnuts
3 tbsp. coconut oil, melted
2 tbsp. agave, rice or maple
   syrup
1 tsp. vanilla extract
1/4 tsp. ground cinnamon
pinch of salt
12 walnut halves, to decorate

Preheat the oven to 350°F (180°C). Grease and line a 9-inch (23-cm.) round cake pan. Put the dates in a bowl, cover with the water, add the baking soda and butter and stir until melted, let cool. Sieve the flours into a bowl, add the baking powder, spices, and lucuma powder and stir to mix. Beat the egg, add the sugar and beat until well mixed. Add the vanilla extract, and stir in the walnuts and almond meal. Pour into the cake pan and bake for 1 hour until browned and springy to the touch.

To make the frosting, blend the ingredients in a food processor. Chill in the refrigerator for 1 hour then spread over the cake, decorate with the walnut halves and store in the refrigerator.

Makes 1 cake

green tea bara brith

see variations page 279

Superfood version of a classic Welsh tea bread, serve with butter or nut butter.

2 tsp. matcha green tea powder or 2 green
    teabags
2 cups boiling water
2 cups mixed dried fruit
1/3 cup coconut sugar or 4 tbsp. agave, maple
    syrup or rice syrup
grated zest of 1/2 lemon

3 cups whole-grain flour
2 tsp. baking powder
2 tsp. pumpkin spice mix
1 large egg

Dissolve the green tea powder in the water, if using tea bags pour the boiling water over the tea bags. Leave to steep for 2–3 minutes and remove the bags. Pour the tea over the mixed dried fruit, sugar and lemon zest. Stir well, cover and leave overnight to soak.

Preheat the oven to 375°F (190°C). Strain the fruit and reserve the "tea" liquid. Put the remaining ingredients in a mixing bowl, beat well to mix then add the fruit and sufficient tea to create a soft dropping consistency.

Grease and line a loaf pan, pour the mixture into the pan and bake for 45–50 minutes until well risen and firm to the touch. Transfer to a wire rack, cool and serve buttered.

Makes 1 loaf

raw raspberry chia jelly

see base recipe page 239

strawberry jelly
Replace the raspberries with 2 cups fresh, hulled strawberries and
1 teaspoon balsamic vinegar to help bring out the flavor.

black currant jelly
Replace the raspberries with 2 cups fresh or frozen and defrosted black
currants, add a little water to thin down the mixture and a little more syrup.

mixed berry jelly
Replace the raspberries with 2 cups fresh mixed berries such as strawberries,
blackberries, raspberries, red currants, black currants, and cherries. Add 1
teaspoon vanilla extract to help bring out the flavor.

superfood peanut butter & jelly sandwich
Spread some homemade or organic peanut butter on a slice of rye,
sourdough or sprouted seed bread, top with one of the raw chia jellies and
serve with some slices of fresh banana for an amazingly healthy snack.

variations

cashew nut butter

see base recipe page 240

peanut butter
Replace the cashew nuts with peanuts, continue as before.

general nut butter
Replace the cashew nuts with almonds, brazil nuts, hazelnuts, pecans, whichever nut you prefer and continue as before.

roasted nut butter
Preheat the oven to 350°F (180°C) line a baking tray with parchment and sprinkle over the nuts of your choice in one layer. Cook for 10-15 minutes, checking and stirring regularly to ensure they don't burn. Continue as before.

mixed nut butters
Blend a variety of nuts such as pecan and cashew, brazil and almond to create your favorite variations. Either process raw or roast and then process to create your own nut butter blends.

salt and sweet variations
Either add 1/2 teaspoon sea salt to the nuts before processing for a salt version or drizzle the finished nut butter with a little honey to sweeten it a little if desired.

variations

raw carrot & orange cake

see base recipe page 243

with lemon
Replace the orange zest and juice with lemon.

with dates
Replace the raisins with 3/4 cup medjool dates, omit the agave as it will be
sweet enough with just the dates.

apple cake
Replace the carrots with 3 peeled apples, omit the pumpkin seeds and
decorate with a few toasted chopped hazelnuts.

zucchini & chocolate cake
Replace the carrots with 2 zucchini, cut into chunks and add 1/4 cup raw
cacao powder. Dust the frosting with cocoa powder and a few cocoa nibs.

variations

carrot muffins

see base recipe page 244

with pecans or walnuts
Add 1/3 cup chopped pecans or walnuts at the same time as the grated carrots.

with sunflower & pumpkin seeds
Add 1/4 cup each of sunflower and pumpkin seeds for extra zinc at the same time as the grated carrots.

with zucchini
Use just one carrot and add one small grated zucchini.

with coconut, raisins & walnuts
Add 1/2 cup shredded coconut, 1/3 cup chopped walnuts and 1/4 cup raisins at the same time as the grated carrots.

freeform plum tart with sweet almond pastry

see base recipe page 247

with peaches
Replace the plums with 6 peaches, chopped, pits removed, and proceed with main recipe.

with rhubarb
Replace the plums with the same quantity of rhubarb, chopped, sprinkle with ground ginger and coconut sugar, and proceed with main recipe.

with apple & cinnamon
Replace the plums with 8 eating apples, peeled, diced and cooked in a little water for 5 minutes to soften. Sprinkle with ground cinnamon.

variations

black bean brownies

see base recipe page 248

with flour to make them lighter
Add 3/4 cup whole-grain or spelt flour and 1 teaspoon baking powder to the mixture.

with beet
Peel and grate 1 raw beet into the mixture.

chocolate orange & hazelnut
Add the zest of 2 oranges and 1/2 cup roughly chopped hazelnuts.

with chocolate avocado frosting & fresh berries
Make up the chocolate avocado mousse, thin out with a little milk, and spread on the top, decorate with fresh strawberries or raspberries.

sweet potato & orange cupcakes

see base recipe page 249

with orange drizzle frosting
Omit the frosting, replace with 1/2 cup superfine sugar and mix with the orange zest and juice, add 1/2 teaspoon ground cinnamon and drizzle over the cupcakes while still warm.

with walnuts
Add 1/3 cup chopped walnuts to the mixture with the vanilla. Walnuts are rich in omega 3 fatty acids, vitamin E, and various minerals.

with cinnamon frosting & pecans
Add 1/3 cup chopped pecans. Omit the frosting, replace with 1 3/4 cups confectioners' sugar, 2 teaspoons ground cinnamon and mix with sufficient water or orange juice to form a thin frosting, drizzle over the cakes once cooled. Top with a pecan half.

with apricots & coconut
Add 1/4 cup chopped dried apricots and 1/2 cup shredded coconut to the mixture with the spices.

variations

kale cupcakes with cream cheese frosting

see base recipe page 250

kale cupcakes with lemon
Replace the orange zest and juice with lemon. Replace the frosting with
lemon juice mixed with superfine sugar for lemon drizzle kale cupcakes.

kale cupcakes with chocolate chips
Add 1/3 cup bittersweet chocolate chips with the orange zest for an orange
chocolate chip version. Replace the frosting with freshly squeezed orange
juice mixed with confectioners' sugar for an orange flavored pale yellow
frosting.

kale, chocolate & beet cupcakes
Omit the orange zest and juice, add a freshly grated beet and a heaped
tablespoon of good quality cocoa powder (raw if possible). Top with the
cream cheese frosting but replace the orange zest and juice with a teaspoon
of vanilla essence.

kale, chocolate & lime cupcakes
Replace the orange zest and juice with lime zest and juice, add a heaped
tablespoon of good quality cocoa powder (raw if possible). Top with the
cream cheese frosting but replace the orange zest and juice with lime zest
and juice.

variations

spelt & seed bread

see base recipe page 253

white spelt loaf
Replace the whole-grain flour with white spelt flour.

walnut and raisin loaf
Omit the seeds and replace with 3/4 cup chopped walnuts and 1/4 cup raisins, cook as before.

with nuts
Omit the seeds and replace with 1 cup chopped Brazil nuts, or whole pecan or macadamia nuts.

variations

kamut bread

see base recipe page 254

seeded kamut
Add 1/2 cup sunflower seeds to the mixture at the same time as the salt.

superseed kamut
Add 1/4 cup sunflower seeds, 1/4 cup pumpkin seeds and 1/4 cup flaxseeds to the flour.

variations

superfood crackers

see base recipe page 257

whole-grain flour version
Replace the spelt flour with whole-grain flour.

oat version
Replace the spelt flour with the same quantity of rolled oats, place these in a food processor and process to a powder, proceed with main recipe.

chili version
Make as above adding 1/2 teaspoon hot chili powder at the same time as the paprika.

blackberry & apple flapjack

see base recipe page 258

with raisins
Omit the apple and blackberries and replace with 3/4 cup flame raisins.

with cranberry & orange
Omit the apple and blackberries and replace with 1 cup dried cranberries or fresh cranberries chopped in a food processor, stir in the grated zest of 2 oranges.

super nutty & seedy flapjack
Omit the apple and blackberries, replace with 2 tablespoons chia seeds, 1/3 cup chopped roasted hazelnuts, 1 tablespoon lucuma powder, 2 teaspoons acai powder, 1/2 cup shredded coconut or coconut flakes, 1 tablespoon flax seed, and proceed with main recipe.

plain flapjack
Omit the fruit, nuts and seeds and proceed with main recipe for a plain version that is still full of slow-release carbohydrates and great to keep you going when active.

variations

granola bars

see base recipe page 261

crunchy version
Omit the bananas and nut butter. Warm 1/4 cup coconut oil in a saucepan with 1 1/2 tablespoons coconut sugar and 1/4 cup runny honey. Once the sugar has dissolved remove from the heat—do not allow the mixture to boil. Stir into the granola and powders and proceed with main recipe.

with cranberry & cherries
Stir in 2 tablespoons each dried cranberries and cherries to the granola.

with sesame, pistachio & rose water
Stir in 2 tablespoons sesame seeds, 1/2 cup crushed pistachios and a teaspoon of rose water to the mixture.

date & walnut cake

see base recipe page 262

coffee, date & walnut
Mix 1/4 cup strong espresso into the dates with the boiling water, proceed with main recipe.

with banana
Reduce the sugar by 1/4 cup and add 2 very ripe mashed bananas to the mixture.

with classic buttercream frosting
Omit the frosting, beat together 1/2 cup unsalted butter, softened, with 2 1/2 cups sieved confectioners' sugar, pulse 1/4 cup walnuts in a food processor until fine and add to the frosting with a little almond or dairy milk if a little thick, decorate with walnut halves.

with lemon drizzle frosting
Mix the juice of two lemons with 2 1/4 cups confectioners' sugar and a little water if too thick, pour over the top of the cake, finish with walnut halves.

variations

green tea bara brith

see base recipe page 264

spelt green tea bara brith
Replace the whole-grain flour with 2 cups whole-grain spelt flour and
3/4 cup spelt flour, proceed with main recipe.

with cranberries & ginger
Replace 1/2 cup dried fruit with 1/2 cup dried cranberries. Replace
1 teaspoon pumpkin spice mix with 1 teaspoon ground ginger and add
4 finely chopped stem ginger pieces to the mixture.

with orange & cinnamon
Replace the lemon zest with the zest of an orange and the pumpkin spice
mix with 2 teaspoons ground cinnamon.

traditional bara brith
Replace the green tea with the same quantity of black tea or use earl grey
or lapsang suchong tea bags to vary the taste. Replace the coconut sugar
with light muscovado sugar.

Alternative ingredient list

Acai powder Omit or replace with acai berries or blueberries or juice if applicable.

Agave syrup Maple syrup, rice syrup or raw sugar such as muscovado sugar.

Almond milk Soy, goat, rice, oat or dairy milk.

Black beans Kidney beans.

Buckwheat flour Wheat flour.

Cacao powder or raw cacao powder Cocoa powder.

Chlorella powder Omit or replace with spirulina, kelp, barley grass or wheatgrass powder.

Coconut oil Butter, melted or sunflower oil except in raw chocolate recipes.

Coconut sugar Agave nectar, rice syrup, maple syrup, demerara sugar or light muscovado sugar.

Coriander seeds Ground coriander.

Cumin seeds Ground cumin.

Giant couscous Standard couscous.

Greek yogurt Greek style yogurt or full fat plain yogurt.

Goji berries Any other dried red berries such as cranberries, cherries, raisins, sultanas or currants.

Lucuma powder Omit or use Maca powder.

Pearl barley Risotto rice.

Pomegranate molasses Balsamic vinegar.

Raw chocolate chips Bittersweet chocolate chips.

Red onion Yellow onion.

Rose harissa Crushed chiles or chile paste, chipotle paste for a smokier flavor.

Spelt flour Wheat flour, preferably whole-grain but otherwise white.

Spelt pasta Standard pasta, preferably whole-grain or gluten-free pasta.

Spirulina powder Omit or replace with chlorella kelp, barley grass or wheat grass powder.

Stevia Agave nectar, rice syrup, maple syrup or light muscovado sugar.

Sweet potatoes White potatoes.

Tenderstem broccoli Broccoli florets.

Whole-grain basmati rice Whole-grain long grain rice or white basmati or long grain rice.

Whole-grain breadcrumbs White breadcrumbs.

Whole-grain flour Plain flour, spelt or rye flour.

Whole-grain pasta Spelt, standard or gluten-free pasta.

Whole-grain tortilla wraps White tortilla wraps or corn tortilla wraps.

index